Ethics
for Real—
People

Ethics for Real People

A GUIDE FOR THE MORALLY PERPLEXED

Loren Broadus

Chalice Press
St. Louis, Missouri

Biblical quotations, unless otherwise noted, are from the *New Revised Standard Version Bible*, copyright 1989, Division of Christian Education of the National Council of the Churches of Christ in the USA. Used by permission.

Cover design: Ed Koehler
Art Director: Michael Domínguez

10 9 8 7 6 5 4 3 2 1   96 97 98 99 00

Library of Congress Cataloging–in–Publication Data

Broadus, Loren,
      Ethics for real people : a guide for the morally perplexed / by Loren Broadus.
            p.   cm.
      Includes bibliographical references.
      ISBN: 0-8272-0809-X
      1. Christian ethics—Popular works.   2. Applied ethics.
3.   Conduct of life.   I. Title.
BJ1261.B76   1996   96-14007
241—dc20   CIP

Printed in the United States of America

Contents

Acknowledgments

Thank God for friends who care enough to criticize us. Many friends, semi-friends, colleagues, and students criticized this manuscript. Fortunately, my critics did not always agree on every idea in the manuscript, so I used many suggestions and ignored others. These people were very helpful, even when they did not agree with each other. They are not responsible for the final product.

The following people read and criticized all or parts of the manuscript: William Barr, Catherine Broadus, Paul Crow, Sharyn Dowd, Colette Horan, Walter Johnson, Michael Kinnamon, Jan Linn, Derek Penwell, and Kevin Phipps. Then it was edited and mailed to Chalice Press. The manuscript was accepted by Chalice Press in a matter of days with a letter from the editor, Dr. David Polk, that said we would discuss the nitty-gritty later. The nitty-gritty turned out to be three single-spaced pages of criticism of the manuscript.

Since I was teaching a course on ethics in the January Interterm of 1995, I distributed Polk's letter to the students for use when reading the unpublished version of *Ethics for Real People*. During the course I redesigned the manuscript and implemented many of Polk's ideas. The twenty-four students, representing four continents and seven church traditions, made significant contributions to the manuscript. I am deeply indebted to Polk and to these students, whose names appear in the appendix.

Lexington Theological Seminary's generous sabbatical program enabled me to research the area of ethics and write this book. For their support in this project I thank the trustees, administrative officers, faculty members, and staff of Lexington Theological Seminary.

I am indebted to the Westwind Coalition of Churches in Kailua, Hawaii, for selecting Catherine and me to serve as "Theologians-in-Residence" in 1993. This unique program is designed to give scholars a setting in which they may be creative and productive while sharing their ideas with the church people in Kailua. It works beautifully.

Carole Davis typed the manuscript more than once. Randy Clay fed the research into the computer for data-collecting purposes.

To all these people: thank you. This is *our* book.

The Banana Festival

Wake's Perch was a small cottage on a hilltop overlooking Fall Creek, a tributary of Lake Cumberland, Wayne County, Kentucky. This was our retreat area. Arthur, Jean, Catherine, and I escaped to this serene setting nestled under the protective branches and leaves of white oak, black oak, post oak, mountain ash, Virginia pine, and tulip poplar trees. The beauty of redbud shrubs and white and pink dogwood trees decorated the scene. Yellow-billed cuckoo birds hid in the treetops and serenaded us, while the redheaded woodpecker furnished the drum sound. The mockingbird charmed us with an occasional concert.

We strolled through the woods, watched lizards do push-ups, listened to the breeze gently fluff the leaves, read articles and books, and dozed off in the hammock. We ate when we were semi-hungry, confessed our small sins to one another, and as Arthur often said, "did our own thing."

It had been a particularly satisfying day, and we were enjoying the gift of silence. Arthur was reading an article on birds, Jean was thumbing through a regional magazine, Catherine was writing a letter, and I was lying on the couch reading a book entitled *Paul's Message and Mission* by William Baird.

In the midst of this tranquillity, I sat up, and with great excitement said, "Listen to this! It's great!" (We all knew Bill

Baird, which assured me that they would be equally impressed with his wisdom.) Then I read:

> An ethic which is grounded in love and faith is naturally harder to observe than a rigid system of moral rules which legalistically prescribes what must be done in every ethical situation. For Paul's ethic, each situation has its own moral demands, and the principle of love is made relevant to different situations in varying ways. Moreover, the situations in which these ethical decisions are made are usually difficult to evaluate. Every situation in life has moral demands and every response has ethical implications; even the decision to do nothing is a moral decision which has responsible ethical results.[1]

I looked up from the book as if expecting applause. Without lifting her eyes from the magazine, Jean said, "We've got to go to the Banana Festival sometime. It's in Fulton." We burst into laughter.

Thereafter, every time one of us talked too academically, abstractly, or made a silly suggestion, we would say, "Let's go to the Banana Festival." It was a gentle formula for bringing us back to reality with laughter.

This book is the result of more than thirty years of searching for some basic answers to life, not just academically, but practically. The search included listening to hundreds of people tell stories of their pains and pleasures, failures and successes, joys and sorrows. Thousands of hours of hearing hopes, dreams, and fantasies, as well as regrets, guilt feelings, and fears, are the backdrop for these ideas. Real people with real problems, which includes all people. Yet the primary people for whom this is written are laypersons and clergy.

Educators, architects, physicians, priests, sanitation workers, sociologists, nurses, business executives, and others attended seminars I conducted. For the past twenty-five years I have been teaching women and men "The Practice of Ministry." Inside and outside class I listen as much as talk. Students have taught and continue to teach me.

Along the way my search has been enriched by reading the Bible and biographies, theology and philosophy, psychology and sociology, and books of fiction and faith. Hundreds of authors have shaped my faith journey.

From 1988 to 1993, several hundred people were interviewed and more than two hundred people filled out a simple questionnaire entitled "Ethics." Hairstylists and health professionals, schoolteachers and scientists, athletes and artists, clergy and counselors, homemakers and high school students, and others, responded to the questions. The computer uncovered some significant and interesting information.

Some older adults still believe everything their parents taught them about the right way to behave.

- Don't lie—tell the truth.
- Don't steal—be honest.
- Don't mow the lawn on Sunday.
- Don't write thank-you notes for wedding gifts too soon after receiving them because people will think you didn't get many gifts.
- Obey authorities.
- Love everyone.
- Men won't marry you if they can get the milk free.

Other adults rejected every mandate given them by their parents.

Before reading on you may find it interesting to write your response to the six questions in the questionnaire on the following page so that you can compare your experience with others' responses.

Oh yes, it seems that most parents teach their children the appropriate condition of their underwear, just in case there is an automobile accident. Can you imagine the physician looking at a bleeding, bruised body in the emergency room of the hospital and shouting in disgust, "Oh my gosh, look at that underwear!" and the father and mother saying, "We're so

ETHICS

1. List the "do's and don'ts" parents, teachers, ministers, and other adults taught you during your childhood.

2. Identify who taught you to think you ought to believe the "do's and don'ts." (Write by each "do" and "don't.")

3. Place a check mark by the ones you still believe.

4. List the three most important ethical issues you face today.

   a.

   b.

   c.

5. List the three most important ethical issues you think others face today.

   a.

   b.

   c.

6. Briefly describe the way you make ethical decisions.

ashamed. We told him to drive slowly and to wear clean underwear. What will people think?"

Edicts and advice to children from their parents always reflect a *value* and often "feel" religious. More about this later.

This book will present both the abstract and practical dimensions to ethics and morality. Using the appropriate authorities, academic ideas and ideals will be presented. An idea *is* practical, because it gives us direction in living.

There are two primary ways this book can assist you in figuring out what to do when confronted with complex ethical issues.

First, throughout the book questions are asked, stories told, authors quoted, and incidents described to help you remember and reflect on your and others' experiences that have moral meaning. You will be challenged to examine and either affirm or reject the moral mandates you received from parents, teachers, clergy, other adults, and communities.

You are invited to remember and reflect on the people who shaped your character (grandparent, teacher, coach, etc.). You will have a chance to recall incidents that made a home in your memory bank. You are encouraged to identify and affirm your ethical ideals for living in a postmodern world.

Second, because ethics/morality is never just a personal matter between "God and me," but a personal, interpersonal, and community concern, a description of how this book may be used in groups—church school classes, study/growth groups, and seminars—is presented. The following are described.

    a. Guidelines for ethics groups
    b. Purpose of an ethics group
    c. Principles for an ethics group
    d. Outline of a sample seminar

I hope that the Banana Festival approach to ethics will keep us in touch with who we and others are becoming as people, committed to making the ideal real in our lives; that is not easy in an age of pluralism that exposes a wide diversity of beliefs about everything, including God. In these times, people are searching for a few absolutes from their authorities—a few truths, rules of living that do not fade into the latest faith fad, pop-psychology clique, or obscure philosophical fantasy. People come to church hoping to get help affirming some values, establishing principles of relating to others, and proclaiming some truths upon which to base their day-to-day living. This book should facilitate that process.

If you wish to discuss any of the ideas in the book or ways to conduct an ethics group, phone me at 606-277-1293.

Note

[1]William Baird, *Paul's Message and Mission* (Nashville: Abingdon Press, 1960), p. 156.

1

The Moral Maze

In the summer of 1991, Barry was rummaging through books, lamps, faded shirts, trousers, dresses, worn-out automobile tires, assorted coffee tables, dishes, and other items usually found at a yard sale. He spotted a used pull golf cart.

"How much for the golf cart?" he asked.

"Twenty dollars," the weekend entrepreneur replied.

"I have only seven dollars on me," Barry bargained.

"Are you lying to me?" the man asked.

"Yes," Barry confessed. "I have fifty dollars on me."

"Are you telling me the truth?"

"Yes! I have fifty dollars in my pocket."

The man stared at Barry, nodding his head up and down ever so slightly, as if in deep thought.

"If you are honest enough to tell me you lied, you can have the cart for seven dollars."

To say that most people are confused about what is ethical and unethical is an understatement. Most people are struggling with what is moral and immoral, what is right and wrong, what is virtuous and evil, what is truth and what is not. People are fighting moral battles over abortion and AIDS, sexism and racism, lookism and ageism, and just about any issue one wants to discuss. Toss the issue into the ring, and people on both sides of the issue will jump into the religious ring to beat their opponents and win the cause for the "real truth." How can two deeply religious people, using what appear to be the same sources of authority (Bible, church tradition), come to opposite positions on abortion or sexism or business ethics or any issue? What is happening to people, institutions, and societies that the subject of ethics has become news—newspaper news, television news, popular news, gossipy news? Has our culture collapsed morally, as some philosophers, politicians, preachers, and parents proclaim?

A major automobile manufacturer sold used cars as new luxury automobiles by disconnecting the odometers so that executives of the corporation could drive expensive models without cost to the corporation—clearly an illegal and unethical act. The press picked up this juicy news item and informed the world of the "dirty deal." It was "damage control time," so the chief executive officer of Chrysler Corporation appeared on television and said, "We did wrong. We should not have done it. We won't do it again."

By repeating the formula many parents teach their children, he became a business cult hero instead of a common criminal, as the owner of Honest Abe's Used Car Lot would probably have been branded. This executive confessed his sins, said he was sorry, promised never to get into the cookie jar again, and he was symbolically carried off on the shoulder of all executives who have to deal with "damage control." "If you are honest enough to tell me you're lying, I'll reward you."

From 1944 until 1951 constant pressure was put upon me by adults to be morally pure because I was an athlete. "Loren, always remember that young people look up to you. You must model the highest moral ideals. No smoking cigarettes. No drinking alcohol. No loose living of any kind." Though I was only sixteen years old when this began, the implication was that the next generation of youngsters would go to hell, society would collapse, and chaos would reign if I led the young astray. Sports figures were supposed to be examples of honesty, responsibility, morality, and respect for others. Things have changed.

In 1990 an article appeared revealing that honesty takes a beating as Colorado wins.

> Who says cheating doesn't pay? Certainly not the University of Colorado football team. Colorado finished No. 1 in the final Associated Press football rankings, giving the university the truly *mythical* national championship...the Buffalos finished with a record of eleven victories, one loss and one tie. But the record should have included two losses, not one.

Here is what happened.

Colorado was playing the last game of the season. They were near the goal line. It was fourth down and time was running out. The Colorado quarterback called the play. The Missouri defense braced for the charge. Tension mounted, the center snapped the ball, and bodies collided. Referees pulled at the layers of players until they found the one with the football. No score. The Missouri players and fans high-fived and hugged each other. In the midst of this confusion, Colorado lined up, ran a fifth play, which is illegal, and scored. The opposing coach complained to no avail; the referees let the score stand and declared Colorado the winner. One would think that the Colorado coaches and most of the football players could probably count to five. The University of Colorado coaches, athletic director, president of the university and the Big Eight Conference remained silent. They let it stand. The National Collegiate Athletic Association was nowhere to be heard.

The article concluded:

> Had Colorado forfeited the victory the school certainly would not have finished first in any poll. All it could have claimed was the distinction of doing the honest thing. And who cares about such trivial matters when there's a national title on the line?[1]

Obviously, times have changed radically in some ways; it seems that truth is taking a beating. John Gardner laments the turmoil surrounding truth when he writes, "Where there is no shame, there is no honor. Shame," Mr. Gardner points out, "is a social emotion. People feel it when they feel they've broken the community's rules. Those who have no sense of membership in any community have no basis for shame."

This editorial claims we are a formless, transient, divided society. "We are quite simply shameless. A survey shows Americans making up their moral code as if values and standards are something you can make up as you go along. This is a kind of moral anarchy."[2]

Though the editorial may overstate the case, in many parts of our society it seems that anything goes; if you don't like the rules, change them to win a national championship or to get elected to political office or to do what you *feel* like doing instead what you should do.

In *The Closing of the American Mind,* Allen Bloom writes:

> There is one thing a professor can be absolutely certain of: almost every student entering the University believes, or says he/she believes that there is not any such thing as an absolute truth.[3]

This is frightening to many people, especially those who not only need to believe in God's absolute moral mandates, but who need others to believe as they do to feel secure in their beliefs.

Though there are different interpretations as to just what it means, all scholars agree that "Reality isn't what it used to be," or seemed to be. That frightens many people.

> The author of a book by the above title points out that the postmodern individual is continually reminded that different people have entirely different concepts of what the world is like. The person who understands this and accepts it recognizes social institutions [church, etc.] as human creations and knows that even the sense of personal

identity is different in different societies. Such a person views religious truth as a special kind of truth and not an eternal and perfect representation of cosmic reality.[4]

According to one postmodern idea, reality is what people tell themselves it is; people do not have the same concepts and stories about reality—how it came into being, how it is now, and what it is to be in the future. Because of the globalization of humankind, we know other people's ideas and stories from all over the world; many of the ideas and stories contradict our understanding of reality, of truths by which to live. What "they" think is ethical and unethical crashes into our safely guarded concepts to deny us the certainty we want.

The fundamental issue for most religious people is the existence of God. In the past these people—Protestants, Roman Catholics, Russian and Greek Orthodox, Jews, and other traditions—held different theological views because of doctrinal differences, church traditions, and personal experiences. They debated the finer points of theodicy, eschatology, forms of baptism, the eucharist, and other salvation issues. *But*, they all agreed that God existed and that God had created some order in the universe with an absolute ethical foundation upon which to build a civilized, caring society.

Globalization challenges this basic assumption about God for many people. One group of postmodern philosophers claims that although there is a cosmic reality, we cannot know what it is, so we make up a story about it to bring some sense to our lives. Other postmodern philosophers claim there isn't any reality "out there"—we are all there is, and even if there is something "out there," we cannot know it, so it does not make any difference either way.

Christians disagree radically. More about this later.

In 1993 William Bennett wrote *The Book of Virtues*. It became a "best-seller" instantly, or so it seemed. The book is designed to "show parents, teachers, students, and children what virtues look like, what they are in practice, how to recognize them, and how they work."[5] The book intends to do this by telling great moral stories illustrating the following virtues.

1. Self-Discipline	6. Courage
2. Compassion	7. Perseverance
3. Responsibility	8. Honesty
4. Friendship	9. Loyalty
5. Work	10. Faith

Bennett's contention that these virtues are a "central part of human nature" met many people's need for absolute truths by which to live.

I decided to test Bennett's thesis. A class of twenty-four clergy from many regions of the United States, Liberia, Hungary, and India was asked to evaluate Bennett's virtues. They were asked to identify the virtues they thought were "a central part of human nature" and to add virtues they thought were absolute—true for all people, in all times, in all places. They were also to discuss these virtues that are culturally communicated and apply to people in that culture but are not necessarily true for all people.

Five groups of five people responded as follows:

- "Though all ten virtues are not of equal value in all cultures, they are innate of human nature—therefore they are valued virtues."
- "Though the majority of my group agreed that Bennett's ten virtues are innate, I would conclude that the only virtue of human nature is the preservation of the species. All of the list of virtues are culturally formed."
- "The following two virtues are absolutes:
  1) Group preservation/community survival is essential to all people and is an absolute.

2) The principle of justice is indigenous to all societies. The specifics of the application of justice is culturally defined.

- "Absolute virtues are love, fairness, and justice. Work and perseverance are not virtues; but self-discipline, responsibility, friendship, courage, and honesty are virtues for us, though they might not be in every culture.

We selected two virtues from the list that are universal:
  1) Friendship, which includes a sense of *affiliation* with others.
  2) Faith in God or a higher Being."

- "We see responsibility and perseverance as universal absolutes based on the necessity to gather food. We see compassion as a possible universal absolute. Add to the list of virtues: altruism, forgiveness, patience, punctuality, and cleanliness."

One group concluded, "Probably the greatest insight gained in doing this exercise was that it is not an easy task to identify what one could consider to be absolute, universal virtues. Welcome to the postmodern world."

Questions for Reflection and Discussion

1. Do you agree with Bennett's list of virtues?

2. Which of the ten virtues do you think are universal (i.e., a part of human nature)?

3. Make your own list of human virtues.

4. Which ones are a part of human nature?

5. Which ones are culturally caught?

It might be helpful to keep your virtues in mind as you continue to reflect on your experience.

Notes

[1] *Lexington Herald-Leader,* Lexington, Kentucky, January, 1990.

[2] *The Wichita Eagle*, May 4, 1991.

[3] Allen Bloom, *The Closing of the American Mind* (New York: Simon and Schuster, 1987), p. 25.

[4] Walter Truett Anderson, *Reality Isn't What It Used to Be* (San Francisco: Harper, 1990), p. 8.

[5] William J. Bennett, *The Book of Virtues* (New York: Simon and Schuster, 1993), p. 11.

2

Who Changed the Rules?

June returned home from college after a stimulating year of study. She had been introduced to the ideas of such people as Carol Gilligan, Lillian Rubin, Rosemary Radford Ruether, Marie Fortune, Walter Truett Anderson, and other creative writers. Excitedly, she told her mother about the new world she had found, her personal freedom from oppressive ideas and systems. Patiently, Martha listened, only occasionally throwing in a gentle rebuttal. This was not Martha's world. She felt very secure in her roles in their small community of 6,000 people. The new ideas made Martha uncomfortable— too much too fast, she thought.

Finally, Martha said, "June, dear, please understand me. I want you to be liberated, but not in my lifetime."

The changes taking place in our world involve us at every level of existence—the international threat of nuclear war, debate about virtues at the local school board meeting, and family values, as Martha experienced with June.

In *The Art of the Novel*, Milan Kundera, a Czechoslovakian novelist and philosopher, was describing Martha's plight when he observed that people desire a world where good and evil can be clearly distinguished, for they have an innate and irrepressible desire to judge before they understand. Religion and ideologies are founded on that desire, he claims.[1] There is much more to religion than that, but that need and desire for a simple, easy way to judge good from evil is threatened by our complex, pluralistic, global community—and rightly so. Life is not, and never has been, as simple as some claim. This is confusing and makes it difficult to figure out how to make ethical decisions.

While philosophers debate cosmic reality concepts, we are confronted with day-to-day living issues that require ethical integrity. Let us view a few more incidents of how change is affecting us and others.

It was reported that in 1992 one million men and women graduated from college in the United States. Unfortunately, there was not a job for every graduate. Disappointment and almost disbelief engulfed many of these idealistic individuals who had anxiously awaited the rewards of their hard work, good grades, and trusting nature. The Protestant work ethic betrayed them.

"I have fifty dollars. That's it. I have to get a job now. I don't have the choice of waiting." She dreaded the thought of working in fast food again.

A young man explained, "I don't understand it. I did what I was supposed to do. I set my goals and worked hard to achieve them. I graduated from college in my field. Now, no job. No future. What am I going to do?" The formula failed thousands of graduates. Who changed the rules?

A few years ago, University of Houston football wide-receiver Torrin Polk said this of Coach Jenkins: "He treats us like men. He lets us wear earrings."[2] The fact that this made the news suggests that someone changed the rules.

Michael Moore, of Rutgers University fame, wrote a how-to manual entitled *Cheating 101*. "Everybody's doing it" was the primary rationale for the book, "so do it right." Some people think that people attend college to get an education; evidently, others think the primary purpose is to graduate. "Since everyone else is cheating, how can an honest student compete, especially for scholarship money based on grades?"[3] Who changed the rules?

Former President Gerald Ford's administration dared to try to get legislature passed that would prohibit the Central Intelligence Agency from assassinating people they thought believed differently from what the C.I.A. considered best for the United States. It shocked a few people that our government did such things. "But everybody else was doing it," so it was explained—assassinating people who believe differently from persons in their government.

During the 1992 Presidential election, one of President Bush's campaign directors not only admitted that he lied about then Governor Bill Clinton, but also stated that lying was good politics. Many of us were taught to trust our country's leaders and believe in an administration based on the "truth, and nothing but the truth, for the people." Some leaders deserve that trust, yet....

In an article entitled "If Truth Be Told, They Are All Lying," James Kirkpatrick concluded: "Truth is taking a beating in this campaign, and we still have two months to go." Both candidates' campaigns contained lies about the other candidate, according to Kirkpatrick.[4]

The nine-year-old daughter of a friend explained to her mother that at school her class was studying the presidential campaign and that she did not know whom to vote for since both candidates were lying. "Vote for the best liar," her mother advised.

A woman interviewed in conjunction with the ethics questionnaire complained about a disgusting suggestion made by the man with whom she spent the night after meeting him in a singles' bar. "Ugh!" she said as she simulated spitting. "He said I could use his toothbrush. Can you imagine anything so disgusting?" Years past, some people thought "one-night stands"—sex with someone you just met and might not see again—was more of a personal, moral issue than using someone else's toothbrush.

There are endless examples of unstable standards reflecting changing rules for relating to one another and institutions in our world.

Though some rules—standards of behavior—have changed, it is obvious that the most significant change is in how much we know about what is really happening in our homes, in our communities, in our country, and all over the world. Politicians did not start lying in 1992, cheating in college was not invented at Rutgers University, all college students have not always found jobs upon graduation. In fact, thousands of hardworking Protestants, Roman Catholics, Jews, and others who believed in the Protestant work ethic lost their jobs in the United States in 1992. The C.I.A. did not invent "unauthorized assassinations of enemies" (at the time of this writing it is officially against the law in the United States), some men have enjoyed wearing earrings for years, and the moral issues of one-night stands have varied from the virtues of virginity to the transmission of diseases orally and otherwise.

Anderson observed that "nobody will be untouched by the postmodern age. For the first time, things are happening to the entire species at once. And we know it. The knowing is one of the most important things that is happening." [5]

Milan Kundera explains:

> The adjective "world" expresses all the more eloquently in the sense of horror before the fact that, henceforward, nothing that occurs on the planet will be a merely local matter, that all catastrophes concern the entire world, and that consequently we are more and more determined by external conditions, by situations that no one can escape and that more and more make us resemble one another.[6]

There is always resistance to the homogenization principle that we "resemble one another." Most of us want and need to belong to a group of people who tell us that we are not only not like others, but that we are better than others in our unique ways. Pluralism contends that we are not fundamentally the same as others, and that is good. We are unique in many ways.

Flannery O'Conner, the novelist, captures the essence of this reaction to the globalization of worldviews in a microscopic setting.

> Mrs. Hopewell had no bad qualities of her own but she was able to use other people's in such a constructive way that she never felt the lack.
> "Everybody is different," Mrs. Hopewell said.
> "Yes, most people is," Mrs. Freeman said.
> "It takes all kinds to make the world."
> "I always said it did myself."[7]

Certainly "most people is different" and it takes all kinds to make the world and it has always been that way, *but now we know it.* That knowing threatens our worldview—that which tells us that though we may not have any bad qualities we can use others' differences from us to prove our superiority. For many that is the function of ethical codes.

This instant awareness of the pluralistic nature of the world evokes different responses. Those who believe that there can be no morals without religion and who need others to believe as they do in order to feel secure in their worldview (beliefs) have to proclaim their truth as absolute. It was reported that the "religious right" had a ten-million-dollar budget to sell its concept of reality and thereby take over politics in the United States. How do these leaders decide that they have the Truth—the absolute Truth?

How do some of the postmodern philosophers know that "Nobody gets to speak for God, nobody gets to speak for American values, nobody gets to speak for nature?"[8] How did Anderson determine that his view of reality was absolutely true in its proclamation of relativity? Religious people are forced to respond to the mass confusion surrounding religious truth, and especially the challenge to ethical standards upon which to build a civilized, caring society.

A World Council of Churches study guide on religious pluralism entitled "My Neighbor's Faith...and Mine" identifies three theological responses to the issue.[9] The first response is the exclusivist approach. There is truth and salvation *only* in Jesus Christ. People who do not confess Jesus as Christ and Savior are lost forever and living in sin.

The second response is the inclusivist approach. Jesus Christ is present and at work even among those who may not know Christ as such. In this view, people of other faiths are included in God's plan of salvation in some mysterious way, through the grace of Christ.

The third response is the pluralistic approach. God can be known in many different ways. God is active with the plurality of the world, and God's saving grace is revealed in many faiths and places.

Because the Christian faith proclaims the love ethic as foundational in revealing the way people ought to relate to one another and how institutions ought to relate to people, these positions are extremely important to issues surrounding religious pluralism. As noted in the study guide:

> In U.S. urban centers and in some smaller communities, people reflecting this pluralism are present in increasing numbers. This reality presents Christians with the need for grounding in their own faith. Local communities of faith will begin to witness the interconnectedness of God's world as represented by differing faiths and ideologies. We do not fear this diversity but welcome the opportunities that will be provided to seek God's will in a world so desperately in need of God's love.[10]

The survival of humankind depends on people of goodwill who have altruistic motives in their dealings with their political systems, religious communities, and neighbors. This is an absolute truth.

Again, the challenge is to find out how to figure out what to do when confronted with highly emotional, complex ethi-

By Whose Authority?

We use our sources of authority to guide us in making ethical decisions. At a particular time we may:

- Appeal to experience—
  "My parents taught me to tell the truth and it has worked for me."

- Appeal to reason—
  "It makes sense to tell the truth."

- Appeal to tradition—
  "My church has believed in telling the truth for centuries."

- Appeal to the Bible—
  "The Bible says always to tell the truth."

cal issues and with other people who do not agree with us on the nature of reality. The following chapters will help us identify the basis upon which we make these decisions—the authorities to which we appeal to assure us that we are right about specific ethical issues.

A major challenge in figuring out how to make ethical decisions is to identify and examine whom or what we are using as a foundation for our decisions. Examining our sources of authority is probably the most practical thing we can do. By locating and affirming what we believe, why we believe it, how it affects us, and who taught us to believe it, we are given the opportunity to choose whom we want to become. In the process, we affirm some ideas/ideals and reject others.

Often we discover that one authority is in conflict with another authority. "The Bible says...and my church says..., but my experience has been totally different." So we use *reason* to make a choice. In a recent article, the author *reasoned* clearly, and drew upon his *experience* of Jesus and his church *tradition* to prove that the *Bible* was the only authority for truth.

Because our experience of life cannot be isolated from our encounter with the Bible, our traditions, and our need for ideas to be reasonable, the different sources of authority will make cameo appearances throughout the book.

When an idea or incident excites or angers you while reading, stop, reflect, and ask, "Why am I responding this way? What is causing me to feel and act as I do?"

Because the chapters are written to evoke responses, to ignite memories, and to encourage reflection on our experiences, each chapter can be used as a basis for discussion in a class, seminar, or workshop. In fact, I have used the process with much satisfaction. See "An Ethics Group: Guidelines" for details.

Questions for Reflection and Discussion

1. Do you believe in the exclusivist position regarding Jesus Christ as the bearer of eternal truth?

2. Do you endorse the inclusivist view?

3. Do you endorse the pluralistic concept of God's activity in the world?

4. What does your position tell you about your list of virtues?

Notes

[1]Milan Kundera, *The Art of the Novel*, translated by Linda Asher (New York: Harper, 1986), p. 7.

[2]"The Last Word," *Lexington Herald-Leader*, Lexington, Kentucky, November 8, 1992.

[3]"Everybody's Doing It," *Lexington Herald-Leader*, Lexington, Kentucky, February 8, 1992.

[4]James Kirkpatrick, "If Truth Be Told, They Are All Lying," *Lexington Herald-Leader*, Lexington, Kentucky, September 9, 1992.

[5] Walter Truett Anderson, *Reality Isn't What It Used to Be* (San Francisco: Harper, 1990), p. 253.

[6] Milan Kundera, *The Art of the Novel* (New York: Harper and Row, 1986), p. 27.

[7] Flannery O'Conner, *The Complete Stories by Flannery O'Conner* (New York: Farrar, Straus and Giroux, 1986), p. 272.

[8] Anderson, p. 183.

[9] "My Neighbor's Faith ... and Mine" in "Toward a Vision of Global Mission: Guiding Principles" (Geneva: World Council of Churches), p. 4.

[10] *Ibid.*

3

To Define Is to Control

John Kennedy Toole, the author of the Pulitzer Prize-winning novel *A Confederacy of Dunces*, also wrote *The Neon Bible*, which he began writing when he was a teenager. The setting of the novel is a small Southern town; the action is seen through the eyes of a fifteen-year-old boy.

David was caught in this small town with a mother who gradually lost touch with reality after the death of her husband in World War II, and with an Aunt Mae who came to care for David and his mother. David's observations of this town's way of living are insightful.

> I knew the way the people in town thought about things. They always had some time left over from their life to bother about other people and what they did. They thought they had to get together to help other people out, like the time they got together about the woman who let a colored man borrow her car and told her the best place for her was up north with all the other nigger lovers, and the time they got the veterans with overseas wives out. If you were different from anybody in town, you had to get out. That's why everybody was so much alike. The way they talked, what they did, what they liked, what they hated. If somebody got to hate something and he was the right person, everybody had to hate it too, or people began to hate the ones who didn't hate it. They used to tell us at school to

think for yourself, but you couldn't do that in the town. You had to think what your father thought all his life, and that was what everybody thought.[1]

David observed that the preacher was the leader who decided what people should hate and what they should think and how they should act. Every year the preacher decided who was to be taken to the "crazy house" and the "poor folks' asylum." He decided, informed them, and benevolently tore them from home, family, and friends for their own good.

The description of a situation determines the ethical issues—what is and what is not acceptable thinking and behavior. The preacher defined the correct code of conduct, who could and could not stay in town. By defining he controlled. Those who define control. Those who control define. One way to control people is by describing the customs of the community, often called *mores*. *The Random House Dictionary of the English Language* defines mores as "folkways of central importance accepted without question and embodying the fundamental moral views of a group."[2]

Mores are the customs, rules, and roles of people in a community that give it stability. Most mores feel moral by the "in-group." This is the way people are supposed to act, and if you don't act the right way, you are out.

The do's and don'ts we receive from our parents have a moral feeling to them. Our parents define what is right and wrong. The family is our first community and definer of proper behavior. From the research with the questionnaire it is apparent that many people think, as Toole described, what their fathers (and mothers) thought, even after becoming "chronologically advantaged"—old. Even those people who reject their parents' advice still remember the words—the do's and don'ts. The messages are forever planted in the mind and are a part of who the person is today.

While visiting in Jacksonville, Catherine, Nettie (Catherine's ninety-two-year-old mother), and I were invited to the Reverend Ed and Elaine Adams' home for lunch. While riding through the speeding traffic of the city, Nettie asked where we were going for lunch. "To Ed and Elaine Adams' home," Catherine answered. "He's a minister, isn't he?" "Yes, Mother, he's a minister, and Ed and Elaine are close friends of ours." "Well," this gracious lady said, "I guess we'll have to watch our language." (Frankly, I hadn't noticed that being a problem with us.)

That prohibition of cursing, of using profanity, in a minister's presence emerged from south Georgia for Nettie about the turn of the century and still lives in the mind of this remarkable woman. It was a double standard of living in that community and still exists in many minds and communities.

Since most people get their "right" way to think and act first from their parents or parental substitutes (grandparents, aunts, uncles, babysitters), these edicts are part of who we are for life. We may ridicule, reject, or affirm the edicts, but they reveal who we have been and who we are now.

In *Slouching Towards Bethlehem* Joan Didion writes, "I think we are well advised to keep on nodding terms with the people we used to be, whether we find them attractive or not. Otherwise they run up unannounced and surprise us, come hammering on the mind's door at 4 a.m. of a bad night and demand to know who deserted them, who betrayed them, who is going to make amends."[3]

After a major conflict at the office, Sarah was visited by the little girl inside her who still needs the approval of others and remembers her mother's saying, "Be nice, darling. People like people who are nice." Sarah feels lonely and angry about this visit.

Bill designs a deceptive advertising slogan for television and is visited by the little boy hearing his mother say, "Always be honest. Tell the truth." There were 2,192 do's and don'ts listed by 212 people in response to the first question on the questionnaire. Of that number 1,661 came from parents, 230 from ministers, and 301 from others (grandparents, teachers, etc.). It is overwhelmingly clear that it is impossible to overemphasize the importance of parents' influence on their children. Of the 2,192 do's and don'ts there were 1,084 ethical issues or mores listed that felt moral.

The parents' edicts fall into two general categories. The first category is general principles of living.

- Do what you are told. (By whom? Everybody?)
- Be good.
- Don't be mean all the time, but you have your times. (How does one decide these times?)
- Be a gentleman/lady.
- Be honest.
- Respect authority—be submissive to authority.

Often the edicts were contradictory.

- Go to war and fight for your country—vs.—Don't kill.
- Love people—vs.—Don't feel or get too close to people.
- Don't have sex, and use protection when you do.
- Do as I say, not as I do.
- Don't do dirty things.

(One woman explained, "I'm 38 years old and still do not know what 'dirty things' are. I asked Mom what dirty things were. 'You know,' she replied. 'No, I don't.' 'Yes, you do, and we won't discuss this again. Just don't do dirty things.' At fourteen years of age I really didn't know what she meant.")

The second category of do's and don'ts are specific instructions for living.

- Don't lie.
- Tell the truth.
- Don't cheat.
- Don't let boys put their hands on your knee; they would not be able to stop.
- Don't hit other people.
- Say "thank you" and "please."
- Send sympathy cards.

As noted, all do's and don'ts are important to children (even adult children) because they *feel* religious in that our sense of well-being relates to pleasing our parents.

Jack is a "nervous wreck" three days before his parents' visit. He knows that his mother will inspect the house for dust and his father will inspect the car for maintenance. Though he has been smoking for ten years, he will not smoke in front of his parents.

Why such behavior for a seemingly emotionally secure, intelligent man? A metamorphosis occurs—adult Jack feels like little Jackie when his parents show up. A visitor from the past. Why this regression?

Though this phenomenon is complicated, one thing is obvious—we do not automatically lose our need for parental approval when we become adults. Our sense of self-worth depends on our parents' feelings for and actions toward us until we deal with these issues openly. The way most children get words of praise ("good boy," "good girl," "I'm proud of you," "You did so well in school," "I love you") is by doing what their parents want them to do and making the parents proud. So morals and mores are paths to parental approval, which translates into "I love you."

Therefore, to disobey our parents is to risk losing their love. To violate the rules and rituals of a community, church, or club is to risk rejection—to lose a sense of belonging. This is one reason mores as well as morals feel religious. Religion has to do with some form of acceptance, approval, affirmation, and salvation.

Questions for Reflection and Discussion

1. Which of your do's and don'ts are morals?

2. Which of your do's and don'ts are mores?

3. Which ones do you want to define as an absolute ethic—a moral mandate for all people all the time?

4. Whom did you think about while reading and reflecting?

Notes

[1]John Kennedy Toole, *The Neon Bible* (New York: Grove Press, 1989), pp. 138–139.
[2]*The Random House Dictionary of the English Language* (The Unabridged Edition), ed. by Jess Stein (New York: Random House, 1971), p. 931.
[3]Joan Didion, *Slouching Towards Bethlehem* (New York: Pocket Books, 1961), pp. 192–193.

4

Dimensions of Ethics

In the fifties young people were promised success if they
followed a formula. The formula was: stay in school, study
hard, go to college, make good grades, graduate, get a job,
work hard, and you will be rewarded with wealth, wisdom,
happiness, and success. So Catherine and I went to college,
graduated, and got jobs. She taught family development at
Fletcher High School, Jacksonville Beach, Florida, and I
taught and coached at Andrew Jackson High School in Jacksonville. Our little attic apartment was located on Beach Bou-
levard in Jacksonville, midway between the two schools. The
formula was working; we were excited about our work and
each other.

About six weeks after we were married, I arrived at the
apartment on a Friday to be greeted by yet another gourmet
meal. Catherine's major was home economics education, so
we had meals that were color-balanced, nutritionally nour-
ishing, taste bud-friendly, and aesthetically presented. The
small table was draped with an off-white tablecloth, candle-
light flickered, and the meal began. After a few bites of food,
hands touched across the table as feet flirted under the table.
The delicious meal was rapidly fading into the background
of my mind. I could not have told you whether I was eating
chateaubriand or collard greens. Catherine must have sensed
the intensity of my passion because she gently squeezed my

hand and said, "You do know that if you ever have an affair, I'll kill you."

We laughed, the chateaubriand or hamburger or whatever it was we were eating reclaimed its flavor, and I do not remember what happened after that.

Catherine's comment is called a heteronomous ethic (but not by many people). Heteronomous behavior is "being good" because an outside authority ordered us to do so. In *Christian Ethics in the Modern Age*, Brian Hebblethwaite of Cambridge University defines a heteronomous ethic as "one which holds that morality is a matter of duties imposed on us from outside by the will of the other."[1]

Most religious people think of ethics as rules of behavior imposed on them by their parents, their teachers, their boss, their church, their government, their group, or some other authority. Even when these authorities seem absent, the mandates for moral obedience remain in our minds and hearts to liberate or oppress us. Our parents live in us through the moral mandates taught to us in childhood and adolescence. When we are "being good" because our parents told us to, our behavior is a heteronomous act. As noted earlier, many adults who responded to the questionnaire embraced every parental rule, others rejected every rule, and still others kept some rules and tossed other rules out as outdated and irrelevant advice.

Some people need more structure—more rules for living—from outside authorities than others do. For these people the instability and uncertainty of social and political structures and the diversity of worldviews by religious authorities are frightening. The cultural and religious pluralism is traumatic for those who want and need an outside authority to tell them that the rules and principles of living are not relative, and that their beliefs are absolute and should be believed by all people everywhere.

These people would agree with the sage of "Lake Wobegon Days," Garrison Keillor. Referring to his religious tradition Keillor wrote, "In the Bible we don't find the word 'maybe' so much, or read where God says, 'on the other hand, uh, there could be other points of view on this.' So we go for the strict truth and let the other guy be tolerant of us."[2]

This confusion is captured in the popular cliché that says, "It doesn't make any difference what you believe as long as you are sincere." Sincerity is a virtue? Or as someone once said, "Acting depends on sincerity. Once you can fake that you have it made." Can you believe that some people believe it does not make any difference what you believe, as long as you are sincere? That is the biggest bunch of nonsense I have ever heard! It makes a difference to me if you believe sincerely that I am your enemy out to hurt you and you have a gun. It makes a difference to me that some religious fanatics support terrorism in the name of God. It makes a difference to me that Catherine believes infidelity in marriage is a major sin punishable by...well, maybe not physical death, but certainly emotional isolation and intimidation, a fate worse than death. Sincerity is not a virtue, even if we fake it. Ill-informed and hostile sincerity destroys. It makes a big difference *what* we believe.

Let us return to the attic apartment incident to assist in identifying four dimensions of ethics that can help us evaluate our ethical ideas/ideals for living. Ethics has been defined as the science of duty, yet it involves much more than objective science and duty, as will become clearer later.

The first dimension of ethics is an *idea* to help us in living. It has to do with thinking. The thought can be held in one's mind. Furthermore, the idea contains within it an *ideal* of behavior. Though stated in the negative side of the idea, "If you have an affair, I'll kill you" contains the ideal of marriage fidelity. The ideal of fidelity supports the idea of faithful relationships that are built on mutual honesty, trust, respect, and love. The idea and ideal are inseparable; they are one.

The second dimension to ethics is the *behavior* proposed to proceed from the idea. For the purposes of this writing, one's actions in relationship to the idea/ideal is termed *morality*. Often there is conflict between what ought to happen and what happens—the ideal versus the real. Through the years, Catherine's words on that romantic evening have remained deeply imbedded in my consciousness along with a keen sense of the consequences of infidelity.

The third dimension of ethics is the *emotional* content. Every idea worth thinking has an emotion riding on its shoulder; that is, we *feel* the importance of the idea/ideal. Emotion carries the idea to the heart of the matter. Catherine's comment carried with it a conviction and, though she spoke softly, her feelings about marriage relationships *were* communicated. There was never any doubt in my mind that Catherine was not making some abstract, interesting philosophical statement. I sensed her strong feelings and realized that the consequences of my being unfaithful would hurt her deeply and that trust, respect, and love would be replaced with hostility, suspicion, and disappointment. Since I also believe in the ideal in question, any violation of it would also create feelings of guilt, shame, and failure for me.

The emotional dimension to ethics has been largely neglected by the church. Many leaders of the church have assumed that all we have to do is tell people what they ought to believe and do, and they can and will follow church orders. This often fails because people need help dealing with the emotional dimension to ethics.

The fourth dimension of ethics is the *motivation* to live what we believe. We can believe in an ideal, feel strongly about it, yet fail to live morally. Where do we get the motivation to live what we believe?

It may be interesting to select one of your most important ethical issues and examine it in relation to the four dimensions of ethics.

The following procedure may help you do so.

Questions for Reflection and Discussion

1. Write simply and specifically your position on the ethical idea/ideal. (Catherine was quite specific.)

2. Image the behavior that the ethical idea/ideal proposes. If you cannot see it happening, it is not specific enough. I could see what I was supposed to do and not to do.

3. Identify the emotions/feelings associated with the idea/ideal: joy, hostility, guilt, shame, compassion, love, etc.

4. Examine who or what helps you live what you believe. Parents, teachers, children, church, Jesus, God, and/or.... You may also discover that which prevents you from living what you believe: fear, need for approval, greed, etc.

Notes

[1]Brian Hebblethwaite, *Christian Ethics in the Modern Age* (Philadelphia: The Westminster Press, 1982), p. 17.
[2]Garrison Keillor, *Leaving Home* (New York: Penguin Books, 1987), p. 28.

5

Pretend Ethics

"I committed high treason, crimes against humanity, and crimes against my own conscience, and I got away with it. I got away with them because I was an American agent all through the war. My broadcasts coded information out of Germany," confessed Kurt Vonnegut's fictional character Howard W. Campbell.[1]

In 1923 Howard was eleven years old when his father, an engineer for General Electric, was assigned to Berlin, Germany. Howard became a playwright in the German language, married a German woman, and continued to live in Berlin. When World War II started Campbell was enlisted by the Nazis to use his skill as a writer to develop and broadcast propaganda; he created and nursed hatred for the Jews. He was a despicable demon of destruction. He was also an agent of the Allies doing his part to defeat the Nazis.

In the introduction to his novel the author, Kurt Vonnegut, Jr., writes: "This is the only story of mine whose moral I know. I don't think it is a marvelous moral; I simply happen to know what it is. We are who we pretend to be, so we must be careful about what we pretend to be."[2]

Campbell was an effective merchant of madness, a person who could fester the hatred of some people against other people. He knew how to prey on the fears and vulnerabilities of frightened people. Campbell was also an agent trying to help the Allies defeat the Nazis. Campbell was who he pretended to be. He confessed that he committed crimes against his own conscience.

Pretending to be something one is not is a common experience for most people and not just for heroes and anti-heroes. In *Self-Help* Lorrie Moore described a common form of pretending—pretending to be one type of person in one setting and another type in a different setting. In the story, the father is a humorous, charming, and talented actor.

> "Your father is a talented man," my mother said, sounding like teachers at school who said similar things to me, my mother sensing our disappointment in never getting his attention for very long. "Talented men have very busy heads. They may seem unkind sometimes...."

> "Cold men destroy women," my mother wrote years later. "They woo them with something personable that they bring out for show, something annexed to their souls like a fake greenhouse, lead you in, and you think you see life and vitality and sun and greenness, and then when you love them, they lead you into their real soul, a drafty, cavernous, empty ballroom, inexorably arched and vaulted and mocking you with its arches. You hear all you have sacrificed, all you have given, landing with a loud clunk. They lock the greenhouse and you are as tiny as a figure in an architect's drawing, a faceless splotch, a blur of stick limbs abandoned in some voluminous desert of stone."[3]

The father pretended to be warm, sensitive, and caring and left the impression of relating to his family in that way. The spouse and daughter were often reminded of how lucky they were to have such a man in their lives. Jacob Fish would say that he did not curse, hit, or physically abuse his family; he simply froze them to death emotionally.

> Speaking to Mr. Fish, my mother cries softly, "Your numbness is something perhaps you cannot help. It is what the world has done to you. But your coldness. That is what you do to the world."[4]

Ethics is what we do to the world, regardless of what the world has done to us. Our conscience is what we received from the world; that is, the result of our experiences. What we do with it is what we do to ourselves and the world. When we do not live up to our ethical standards and make it appear otherwise to others, we feel guilty, disappointed in ourselves, and shameful. When we pretend to be what we are not, our conscience punishes us by saying, "Yes, you are that way." Campbell did not get away with his crimes of conscience; he knew what he did was evil and felt the sting of a guilty conscience. Jacob Fish lived the deception he perpetuated and consequently lived the life of an emotional zombie. It cost him the rewards of intimacy.

We have a conscience filled with do's and don'ts created by our parents, peers, church, and other people and institutions. At times, we *pretend* to be what we and our community (church) wish we were for at least two reasons.

First, we believe that who we are is not good enough; we do not live up to our community's standards. Roland is the minister of a congregation in a town of 6,000 people. I know Roland as a calm, peaceful, quiet, and concerned person. He demonstrates his commitment to people through his soft pastoral skills. His Rogerian nondirective approach to people leads them to think that he is a sensitive, attentive, and caring father and spouse.

"Loren," Mary said, "the minute the doors to the manse close, Roland changes. Some kind of metamorphosis occurs...."

I waited for her to continue; this was difficult for her.

"He is mean, cruel, and calloused. He shouts at us—the children and me—cruel words, and the tone of his voice sounds like he wants to kill us....I'm really scared."

"Does he hit you?"

After a long pause and choking back her tears, Mary said, "I've never told anyone any of this. You have to promise me that you won't tell."

"Tell me about the beatings."

"He beats me and the children; he loses control."

She begins to sob. "We can't leave him; we don't have any place to go."

Roland pretends to be kind because the Christian community says that is what a person ought to be, especially a minister. Roland *is* kind to townspeople and parishioners; that is who he is. He is also an abusive person to his family; that is who he is.

Roland pretends to be a kind person and gives the impression that he is a fine father and husband because if he treated parishioners as he does his family, he would not only lose his job; he would also be arrested for assault and battery. (Violence in the family will be explored later.)

The second reason people pretend to be what they think they are not is the need for approval. Roland needs the townspeople to like him and praise him for his kindness. His sense of decency comes from doing kind deeds, even though he may resent the very people he helps. He needs people to approve who he pretends to be, not only for job security, but for psychological reasons.

He needs to belong; and to be accepted as a member of the community he has to either believe in and live by its moral code and mores, or to pretend to do so. Roland lives with the conflict of who he pretends to be and who he thinks he is not. He feels like an impostor, and this eats away at his integrity and sense of self-worth. He is ashamed of himself. (Let's hope he becomes who he pretends to be.)

"Hypocrite" is the word often used to describe such behavior. Hypocrisy is an ethical issue in most communities. "It is a pretense of having a virtuous character, moral or religious beliefs and principles that one does not possess. A pretense of having some desirable or publicly approved attitude."[5]

There are two levels of hypocrisy. The first level occurs when a person deliberately plots to deceive people, as Roland does. In Matthew 6:1–2 Jesus warns, "Beware of practicing your piety before others in order to be seen....So whenever you give alms, do not sound a trumpet before you, as the hypocrites do in the synagogues and in the streets, so that they may be praised by others."

The second level of hypocrisy occurs when people do not know they are deceiving. In Luke 6:41–42, Jesus preaches, "Why do you see the speck in your neighbor's eye, but do not notice the log in your own eye? Or how can you say to your neighbor, 'Friend, let me take out the speck in your eye,' when you yourself do not see the log in your own eye? You hypocrite, first take the log out of your own eye, and then you will see clearly to take the speck out of your neighbor's eye."

In a society suffering from moral anarchy, there needs to be increased awareness of what is and what is not acceptable behavior. We need some sense of community norms (morals and mores) so that we will know what to pretend to be. We also must hold our communities accountable. Sometimes the community pretends to be what it is not. A church may claim to love all people while perpetuating racism or sexism or classism or nationalistic chauvinism.

The Christian faith stresses that we should act morally, be responsible in interpersonal relations, and try to do the loving thing, regardless of how we feel about people. Christian love is more than a feeling; it is behavior. A friend said, "I'm going to quit *shoulding* on myself." Not only is that unrealistic, it is not possible or desirable in our complex society, and my friend knows that. The Christian faith has a dimension of "shouldness" to it; it offers perimeters of behavior so that people may live creatively in community.

So when we pretend to care by performing a kind deed, that action is not to be condemned. When we speak on behalf of an oppressed group with whom we disagree over some of the people's words and behavior, that action is not to be condemned. We can affirm and criticize at the same time. Healthy relationships do that.

The so-called hippie subculture of the sixties (now baby boomers) universally condemned their elders for being phony, for pretending to be what they were not. It is not phony when you do not want to help someone, and in fact do not like him or her, yet you do help that person. It is not phony to want to have an affair with someone at the office, and pretend not to, thereby resisting the temptation.

In a seminary class, John described a parishioner who was insensitive, had a caustic tongue, and used it as a weapon. She constantly criticized John. After about ten minutes of describing and berating this sixty-year-old woman, he confessed that he did not like the woman.

"Can you understand that? I don't like her, but I love her and want to help her. Can you understand that?"

"Sure," Marsha replied. "I have teenagers."

The Christian community proclaims an ethic that says you do not have to like, and you do not have to want to do the good deed, in order to live morally.

Rational Behavior Therapy operates on the premise that in order to live responsibly and to take charge of your life you must image who you want to be. You decide how you want to relate to people and manage your life. You do what you think you should do to become who you want to be, regardless of how you feel. By pretending—repeating this behavior over and over—it begins to feel natural and not phony. We gradually become the person we think we want to be.[6]

Maybe a third reason we pretend to be what we are not is because we want to become more than we have been. We cannot help our numbness or our fears or our phobias the world gave to us; that is our experience. We can pretend to be more, not less, than we are while pursuing a higher ethic. Motivation is the gauge of the ethical barometer. Are we pretending primarily to deceive people without any intention of changing, or are we pretending to try to live up to a high ideal of ethical behavior hoping to become more fully the person we pretend to be, or a little of both?

Aristotle expressed this idea many centuries ago. "We become just by doing just acts, temperate by doing temperate acts, brave by doing brave acts."[7]

We are who we pretend to be, so we must be careful about who we pretend to be.

We have to decide who we want to become as well as identify who we were programmed to be by our parents and others. By deciding who we want to become, we may choose the behavior we want to manifest. This will give us guidance in making ethical decisions.

Questions for Reflection and Discussion

1. Who do you pretend to be?
2. Do you act the same way at home as at work or church?
3. Who do you want to pretend to be?

While writing that last question I remembered a childhood experience of pretending. My mother evidently was worried about her son who thought a lot and often did not notice or speak to people. Being unfriendly was a sin to her. So she would "walk me" around the neighborhood and say, "Here comes Sonny. Speak to Sonny." "There is Mrs. Lammons on the porch; speak to her." We did this drill for weeks. Evidently it worked. Some people think she overdid it.

Notes

[1]Kurt Vonnegut, Jr., *Mother Night* (New York: Harper & Row, 1961), p. v.
[2]*Ibid.*, p. 34.
[3]Lorrie Moore, *Self-Help* (New York: The New American Library, 1985) pp. 30, 36.
[4]*Ibid.*, p. 30.
[5]*The Random House Dictionary of the English Language* (New York: Random House, 1971), p. 701.

⁶Maxie C. Malltsby, Jr., *Help Yourself to Happiness Through Rational Self Counseling* (Boston: Esplanda Books, 1975).

⁷Aristotle, *Nicomachean Ethics*, II. 1. 4-5, translated by H. Rackam, Loeb Classical Library, Vol. 19 (Cambridge: Harvard University Press, 1926, Reprint 1982), p. 73.

6

Cardboard Butterfly Values

In *The Writing Life* Annie Dillard tips us off to this tidbit of trivia.

> An intriguing entomological experiment shows that a male butterfly will ignore a living female of his own species in favor of a painted cardboard one, if the cardboard one is big. If the cardboard one is bigger than he is, bigger than any female butterfly ever could be, he jumps the piece of cardboard. Over and over again, he jumps the piece of cardboard. Nearby, the real, living female butterfly opens and closes her wings in vain.[1]

Some people prefer the cardboard life of television to the real people opening and closing their wings for attention.

Eleanor was the mother of two small girls, ages six and four. She was concerned about Ellen. "Every day, when Ellen and I watch *Days of our Lives*, she cries."

"Tell me about it," I urged her.

Eleanor described the history of the soap characters, the current conflict they were having, and her analysis of what she thought was going to happen next. While talking she vacillated between cheerfulness and sadness, almost breaking into tears at times.

"Do *you* cry during the program?"

"Well, yes...sometimes."

"What specifically is the problem?" I asked.

"I'm worried about what kind of psychological damage this might do to Ellen," she explained. "It's not healthy for a four-year-old child to be that emotionally upset every day.... What should I do?"

I thought to myself—I know the answer to this problem. "Stop watching *Days of our Lives*," I wisely advised.

Her mouth fell open, her eyes glared at me, as she shook her head from side to side. "I couldn't do that!" she said in almost disbelief that I could be so insensitive.

Eleanor explained that she and her mother watched the program when Eleanor was a little girl and that she could not stop watching the soap opera of her life. She reviewed for me the drama in progress between two of the characters. She was more involved emotionally with these people than the real people in her life. The cardboard characters gave her a feeling that she was alive; she experienced a wide range of emotions; she fought battles, made love, and remained beautiful while in bed. She was the victim of someone else's imagination.

Eleanor jumped the cardboard butterfly, but she was not the only one to do so. This small town had a whole network of people who talked about characters on the soap opera as if they were real people. The television drama was a part of hundreds, if not thousands, of people in that town.

The factory workers, men and women, watched the soap opera during lunch break. When two characters on television were getting married, the factory workers held a reception with a wedding cake and punch, adding to the festive occasion for the workers.

This was a central part of their community. The soap opera offered people a fantasy life that was shared. Five days a week it affected these people's thoughts, feelings, and behavior. This television cardboard community was real for these people and it touched others who lived in the town. Eleanor, who was not a member of the church I served as pastor, came to see me with her problem because the character in the soap with whom she identified most went to see a minister for counsel. I, also, became a bit-part player in this expanding drama.

After describing the seductiveness of movies, Annie Dillard concluded, "Even knowing that you are manipulated, you are still as helpless as the male butterfly drawn to painted cardboard."[2]

We are constantly manipulated and challenged by communities that give us experiences that determine our values—our ideas/ideals, our ethics. In *Bible and Ethics in the Christian Life*, Bruce C. Birch and Larry L. Rasmussen explain:

> What we are able to discern and do results from our participation in various communities. A variety of social worlds has shaped us, determined our general bearing in life, even engineered our specific responses to particular issues. We cannot and do not muster moral insight for ourselves by ourselves apart from our communities, any more than we are or can be human beings apart from others. Everything we know about morality and the moral life, or anything else, for that matter, is finally a community enterprise and achievements. While it is true that individuals are not simply community clones, they are unique, and may well arise above the moral level of their communities, it is true with equal force that even the most private decisions and achievements are the results of our social experience and could neither exist nor be understood apart from that experience.[3]

Which communities influence us? Which ones influenced our parents? Where did these "values" originate to filter into the family fabric? The do's and don'ts were probably not original with our parents. Can we distinguish the painted cardboard butterfly from the real things? Obviously, what is a painted imitation for one person is the real thing for another.

In Colorado City, Arizona, a fourteen-year-old boy was reprimanded by his principal and sent home to change a shirt that offended the teachers, students, and principal of the school. The shirt depicted the Penguin, Batman's archenemy. The boy's mother took the shirt to school, marched into the principal's office and said, "Lawrence, how does this shirt affect my boy's education?"

The mother continued, "He just looked at me and said that it's a sign of devil worship."

The superintendent of Colorado City schools defended the school district's dress code as being "as liberal as it can be. Clothes aren't allowed that depict obscenities, immodestly expose the body...."

Two years before that incident the fourteen-year-old was harassed by teachers and students for wearing a short-sleeved shirt.

These people know who they are by the strict rules of conduct that tell who belongs and who doesn't, who is good and who is evil. The shirt, the dress code, tells who is moral and who is immoral.

The Roman Catholic Rule of St. Benedict is highly structured for the monks. In addition to detailed instructions on worship, work, weekly kitchen service, and other duties and principles, there are seventy-two rules called "the instruments of good works." The rules are both general—"to love one's neighbor as oneself"—and specific—"to visit the sick."

In the monastery, the abbot has "the obligation to love his sons, the monks, and to exercise his love by encouraging and assisting them in their quest for God and perfection. Since the monks were to be sons in Christ to the abbot, they owed him obedience in all things, in St. Benedict's as in Augustine's opinion. The difference seems to be that while Augustine saw obedience as one virtue among many, with love as the most important, Benedict saw obedience as the single reality, the master virtue."[4]

Obedience, a basic principle of monastic life, is a virtue upon which the community survives, according to this religious order. Some people unfamiliar with this monastic order might think that obedience is a cardboard butterfly and that many of the rules that govern their lives fall into that same category. The difference is the monks understand why they do what they do and believe that these rules are the real thing lived in the Presence of God.[5]

Contrast this tradition with the rules at Aldersgate, a United Methodist Retreat Center in eastern Kentucky. The rules of being a part of this community are precise. As Lee Wallace-Padgett, the camp director, said, "The rules have to be simple and clear. No room for misunderstanding, because teenagers will interpret vagueness to their wants and wishes."

ALDERSGATE HOUSE RULES

1. No smoking.
2. No littering.
3. Don't sit on the Ping Pong table.
4. No rock throwing.
5. Aluminum cans go in separate trash cans.
6. Conserve water.
7. No boys in girls' cabins; no girls in boys' cabins.
8. Help out with cleanup.
9. Respect and love each other.
10. Obey the rules.
11. Have fun.

After reading these rules, Jane, about thirty-five years old, said, "The last rule is made impossible by the first ten."

The motivation and reason for the rules of living seem to be a factor in the ethics/morality drama. The Benedictine monks understand that rules are established for their and the community's benefit, and obedience to these rules is a virtue. There is a theological rationale for obedience.

Many teenagers who attend camp at Aldersgate probably think that obedience is a cardboard butterfly to be challenged and is not for real people. The teenager in Colorado City did not think obedience to the dress code (cardboard butterfly?) was necessary, and he did not understand why such rules existed.

Response to the ethics questionnaire and interviews with the responders shed some light on the issue. When children (and adults) know *why* they are supposed to act a particular way they are less likely to be resentful of the rule, though they may dislike it. More important, the motivation of the parents in establishing and enforcing the rules (do's and don'ts) is a significant factor in the person's moral development.

When I was a child, my parents repeatedly warned me not to go within one block of the river. "The river is dangerous and you could drown if you fall in." Hardly a day passed from the years seven, eight, and nine of my life that I did not visit the river either to fish or swim.

The police arrested me and my friends for swimming in the river. They booked us, put us in jail, and phoned our parents. That entire summer was spent on one block; I was prohibited from crossing a street. I regretted the punishment. I did not resent it or my parents for punishing me. I understood both why the rule existed and that it was primarily for my benefit.

Following are some of the resented parental mandates:

- Do it because I say so.
- Don't embarrass your parents.
- Don't question my advice.
- Respect your elders no matter what, even if they are wrong.
- Don't do anything the neighbors will gossip about.
- As long as you live under your parents' roof, they are the authority.
- Never question what an adult says.

The above mandates are family mores and "morals" created to benefit the parents more than the children. Parents who control their children with unreasonable and unexplained "moral" demands raise rebels who resent authority. For these parents obedience seems to be a "virtue," created for their comfort.

When families, communities, and churches have rules of ritual and behavior that must be obeyed without question, and seem to exist for the survival, safety, satisfaction, and security of the institution and its leaders and not for the welfare of "real people," resentment and disrespect rise to challenge or the people abandon the community, family included.

In the "Do-it-because-I-say-so" regime, expressions such as "I'm doing this for your own good" and "This hurts me more than it does you" are not believed because the rules feel like cardboard butterflies created to seduce or distract people from the real thing.

Questions for Reflection and Discussion

1. Did your parents and other adults say, "Do it because I say so," or did they explain why you were supposed to act a particular way?

2. What were the rules in your family when you were a child?

3. What are the rules now that you make them?

4. How did you decide the rules? For whose benefit?

5. What are the rules of your community? Your church?

6. What is your response to these rules? Why?

Notes

[1]Anne Dillard, *The Writing Life* (New York: Harper Perennial, 1989), pp. 17–18.

[2]*Ibid*, p. 18.

[3]Bruce C. Birch and Larry L. Rasmussen, *Bible and Ethics in the Christian Life* (Minneapolis: Augsburg, 1989), pp. 17–18.

[4]*The Rule of St. Benedict*, translated by Anthony C. Meisel and M. L. del Mastro (New York: Doubleday, 1975), p. 30.

[5]Having had the opportunity to know, visit, and worship with monks at Gethsemane Monastery and having taught at St. Meinrad Monastery Seminary, I have grown to appreciate this rich tradition.

7

Santa Claus Ethics

"Have you been a good little girl?" asked Santa Claus. "Have you been a good little boy?"

This obese person dressed in red and white wearing a long white beard promises to bring children bicycles, Power Rangers, computer games, and other gifts if the children have "been good." Some families perpetuate the myth that if you have misbehaved by failing to say "thank you," "please," or "I am sorry," and if you shout, pout, or mistreat your brother or sister or disobey your parents, Santa Claus will do one of two things—not give you any toys (kiss the bicycle good-bye) or bring you switches instead of toys (and we know how switches are used).

From this Santa Claus myth, we see an anthropology that is detrimental to the emotional and spiritual health of children and adults. Millions of people think of God as a type of Santa Claus. We must act morally so that God will reward us with health, happiness, and prosperity.[1] If we are evil—act bad—God punishes us with disease, death, and poverty. This is not only pathetic psychology, it is terrible theology. Small children tend to put all authority in the same category—parents, teachers, Jesus, God and Santa Claus.

Lawrence Kohlberg lists six developmental stages of moral growth.[2] Though there is some disagreement with his theory, the first stage of development certainly describes Santa

Claus Ethics and millions of people who believe in a God who acts like Santa Claus.

Stage I is the obedience and punishment belief. We must obey authority (i.e., God) in order to avoid punishment. Avoidance of punishment and pleasing those in power are values in their own right, and are the motivations for moral behavior in Stage I. There is a lack of understanding of, or respect for, an underlying moral order.

What is our motivation for being good, acting morally? Several years ago Andy, my brother, and I were discussing our father.

"He's amazing, isn't he, Bubba?" Andy said.

"He sure is," I replied.

"How does he do it?" Andy asked. "We're seventeen years apart in age and have the same value system: family first, truth at all costs, don't cheat, take turns, be patient with people....So many ideas filtered to both of us, and I can't remember any specific words he spoke about ethics. Amazing."

"The next time I see him I'll ask him," I promised.

Since all three of us lived in different states it was six months before I was with my father.

"Pop, Andy and I were discussing how ethical you have always been. When you ran for political office and were offered a bribe that would have solved your financial problems, you turned it down. You always seem to do the right thing. How do you do it?"

I had waited six months for this profound philosophical foundation for character. Pop looked at me, glanced back at his easel, and continued painting as he thought about the question.

"Fear," he said without missing a stroke of the brush.

"FEAR! That's *it*?" I said, as I burst out laughing.

"That's it."

Of course, there is more to his moral character than fear; but fear was one way to determine what action should be taken—Stage I—obedience and punishment.

"I have to go to bed with myself every night," he said, "and I try not to do anything that would cause me to lose sleep."

His conscience is his guide; fear and potential guilt feelings are his motivator at one point in the process. The fundamental motivation for acting morally is his drive to live up to *his* expectations of who he thinks he ought to be, thereby he is rewarded with self-respect and a good night's sleep when he lives up to his ethical standards.

Some of the people responding to the assignment "Briefly describe the way you make ethical decisions" stated that their conscience was a big factor in making ethical decisions.

Is conscience an effective indicator of what is right and wrong, good and evil? It depends on who built the conscience and the content of this historical reservoir of do's and don'ts. Let us examine this experience.

There has been more nonsense written about conscience by otherwise reasonable people than probably any other subject except God. Consider the following quotes. Excuse the sexist language.

> "What is moral is what you feel good about after and what is immoral is what you feel bad about after."—*Ernest Hemingway*

> "The moral experience of man has everywhere and in all places been the same."—*John Haymes Holmes*

> "I simply want to please my own conscience, which is God." —*Gandhi*

> "An Englishman thinks he is moral when he is only uncomfortable." —*George Bernard Shaw*

> "The Anglo-Saxon conscience does not prevent the Anglo-Saxon from sinning; it merely prevents him from enjoying his sin." —*Salvador de Madariaga y Rojo*

> "Conscience is the inner voice that warns us somebody may be looking." —*Henry Louis Mencken*

Each of the following quotes challenges us to think about living with ourselves.

"Conscience is the voice of the soul, as the passions are the voice of the body. No wonder they often contradict each other." —*Jean Jacques Rousseau*

"Man's conscience is the supreme judge of what is true or false, good or evil. A person who lives professing a belief he does not hold has lost the only true, the only immutable thing—his conscience."—*Dagobert David Runes*

"Conscience is merely our own judgment of the right or wrong of our actions, and so it can never be a safe guide unless enlightened by the word of God."—*Tyron Edwards*

"Conscience, which ought to confront us with our real sins, is commonly used to distract our attention from them and to center it on less important matters." —*Harry Emerson Fosdick*

From the philosophers we receive these words.

"We cannot live better than in seeking to become better, nor more agreeable than in having a clear conscience." —*Socrates.*

"There is no witness so terrible—no accuser so powerful as conscience which dwells within us."—*Sophocles*

"He will easily be content and at peace, whose conscience is pure."—*Thomas à Kempis*

"Conscience is justice's best minister. It threatens, promises, rewards, and punishes, and keeps all under its control....While conscience is our friend, all is peace, but once offended, farewell to the tranquil mind." —*Lady Mary Wortley Montagu*

"The torture of a bad conscience is the hell of a living soul." *John Calvin* (Just like Calvin.)

"A clear conscience is a perpetual Christmas." —*Ellis Young, my father-in-law*

"Conscience tells us that we ought to do right, but it does not tell us what right is—that we are taught by God's word."
—*Henry Clay Trumbull*

It is not as simple as Trumbull believes. Even those who claim to know "God's word" do not agree on the right moral action. As noted earlier, our conscience depends on who built it and that usually points to parents and other adult authorities. These adults reflect the culture, with its morals and mores, of a particular place and time and religion. So people motivated by conscience to do good can be in conflict with others who are also following their conscience.

A coal miner from eastern Kentucky said, "I would rather be dead than cross a picket line." The middle-aged minister said, "There is no way I'll mow the lawn on Sunday. It's a matter of conscience." A drifter stabbed a woman several times. He took off his shoes at the back door before entering the house. "My mother taught me not to track mud in the house. I couldn't have dirtied the woman's kitchen floor." He felt no remorse for killing the woman. With the conscience, fear of guilt feelings and punishment is one phase of moral motivation. Another phase is the anticipation of feeling good about ourselves for living up to our ethical standards.

In *The Serenity Prayer* William J. Pietsch explains, "The conscience is a very sensitive inner gauge that measures—based on the information we have—how far we are from the highest values we know. As we move away from our highest values pain increases, pain lessens as we move toward acceptance of our highest values."[4]

Conscience must have a context. Our conscience was built by people who lived in some kind of culture-community. We need a community of people to stir the content of our conscience and help guide us with our moral actions even when our conscience is at peace with itself, especially in the face of injustice. The church serves such a function.

In *The Devil Tree* by Jerry Kosinski, one character says: "It seems that what I really need is a drug that will increase my consciousness of others, not myself."[5]

Maybe the issue is not so much how I can be content—have inner peace—but what I can do for others that will help them. Maybe the best thing that can happen to many of us is to be uncomfortable with ourselves for the right reasons.

A clear conscience may not be the loftiest goal in life or the strongest motivator for doing good.[6]

Questions for Reflection and Discussion

1. Review your responses to the second question on the ethics questionnaire. Identify who taught you to think you ought to believe the do's and don'ts.

2. Was your childhood God more like Santa Claus than Jesus? If so, how? If not, how?

Notes

[1]During a tent meeting in the fifties in Jacksonville, Florida, Oral Roberts pointed to his shirt and said "If you accept Jesus, you too can wear silk shirts." That didn't sound like too much of an inducement for my mother.

[2]Lawrence Kohlberg and Thomas Lickona, *The Stages of Ethical Development: From Childhood Through Old Age* (San Francisco: Harper, 1986).

[3]Most of the quotes on conscience came from *The International Dictionary of Thought*, compiled by John P. Bradley, Leo F. Daniels, and Thomas C. Jones (Chicago: Ferguson Publishing Company, 1969), pp. 159–162. Some quotes emerged from my memory without any specific bibliographical data.

[4]William J. Pietsch, *The Serenity Prayer* (San Francisco: Harper and Row, 1990), p. 30.

[5]Jerry Kosinski, *The Devil Tree* (New York: Henry Holt Company, 1973), p. 67.

[6]For an interesting discussion of conscience see *Conscience in the New Testament* by C. A. Pierce (London: SCM Press, 1955).

8

Enlightenment, Reason, Religion

"I think, therefore I am."—*Descartes*
"I don't think, I *know.*"—*James*
"I don't think I know, either."—*Bubba*

The above comments raise the issue of reason—thinking—in the search for truth, for ethical ideas/ideals upon which to base our lives. The place of reason in solving humankind's problems of peace, prosperity, poverty, and prejudice range from those who believe in the possibility of the Enlightenment's promise of reasoning our way into social and political utopia to the fundamentalist who says "I don't think, I *know,*" which makes a mockery of Kierkegaard's leap of faith.

Because it is impossible to overestimate the influence of the Enlightenment on our search for truth, we will explore *briefly* some of the ideas generated by that movement. Albert Camus' novel *The Stranger* introduces the topic.

"Mother died today. Or, maybe, yesterday; I can't be sure." Those are the opening words of Albert Camus' novel *The Stranger.*[1] Monsieur Meursault, hereafter referred to as "M," left Algiers to attend his mother's wake and funeral, some fifty miles from Algiers.

At the wake, M smoked cigarettes, drank coffee, and did not act sad. No tears. The day after the funeral M decided to go to the swimming pool. It was Sunday. He met Marie there, they swam together, with a little romantic touching. They went to dinner, then saw a humorous film, followed by an erotic conclusion to a romantic day at M's apartment.

After dating M for awhile, Marie asked him if he wanted to marry her.

"Either way is all right with me," M answered.

"Do you love me?" Marie asked.

"No."

"Then, why marry me?"

"Because you want to. Either we get married or we don't. It doesn't make any difference to me."

M's boss offered him a job in Paris; a significant promotion—more money and prestige. Paris was a wonderful place to live. The boss was excited about this gift to M.

"OK," M responded.

"What do you mean, OK?"

"Either way is all right with me."

M was walking on the beach with a gun in his pocket, when he came upon an Arab sunning. M recognized the man as the person who had cut his friend with a knife in a fight. The man moved; it looked as if the sun reflected on the blade of a knife. M shot the man, paused, and then shot him four more times. At his trial, he could not explain why he shot the man four times after the first shot.

"The prosecuting attorney began by summing up the facts, from my mother's death onwards," M explained. "He stressed my heartlessness, my inability to state my mother's age, my visit to the swimming pool where I met Marie, our matinee at the pictures where a Fernandel film was showing, and finally, my return with Marie to my room."

When M told the magistrate that he did not believe in God, the magistrate plumped down into his chair indignantly. "That is unthinkable," he said. "All men believe in God, even those who reject him." Of this he was absolutely sure; if ever he came to doubt it, his life would lose all meaning.

M is the type of person imaged and feared by the critics of those who use reason as an ethical authority. M appears to be amoral; traditional Christian morality is not a factor in his life. He is emotionally cold, stoic, and without compassion. The idea that someone could be moral, compassionate, and loving without believing in God threatens the critic's faith. The magistrate knew that all people believed in God; it was unthinkable to think otherwise. The magistrate's faith and meaning depended on others believing as he did. "Do you wish," he asked indignantly, "my life to have no meaning?" Later in the novel the chaplain has a similar encounter with M when M refuses to call upon God, even in the face of execution.

The people who believed in God tried and convicted M for murder, not because he killed a man, but because he appeared heartless—he didn't care about people—he did not grieve his mother's death. He did not believe in God.

In *Resistance, Rebellion, and Death*, Camus writes, "If Christianity is pessimistic as to man [people], it is optimistic as to human destiny [heaven]. Well, I can say that, pessimistic as to human destiny, I am optimistic as to man."[2]

The Enlightenment thinkers were optimistic that humankind could think its way into truth—utopia—and solve the major social, political, and moral problems. They "believed the world would achieve constant improvement if people would use their rational minds to scrutinize social beliefs mercilessly and throw them away like worn-out shoes when no longer needed."[3] "Each individual was thought to possess within his or her own self-sufficient rationality the ability to discover the truth, know the good, and make informed moral judgments."[4]

The Enlightenment attempted to exorcise morals from religion and place the responsibility for a better world in the hands of people without God's help. In many instances, "God did not create people, people created God," and God failed to deliver the people from their problems; so reasoned some philosophers then and now.

Religious leaders shouted from the pulpit and the classroom—"The Enlightenment failed, look at where we are—poverty, wars, unjust political systems, prejudice, ethnic cleansing, and other failures of humankind to reach that elusive utopia." Yet, those who reason against reason as a source for their religious faith are fighting a battle that is no longer relevant by people who know that the enlightenment is not the issue. Most of us know that we cannot reason ourselves into emotional, intellectual, and ethical whole people. However, reason has a place in our faith and in our search for answers to complex ethical problems. Reason is a response to fideism.

Fideism refers to the attitude that regards belief as a sufficient substitute for knowledge, that says: "My own belief is good enough for me and you; don't confuse me with your facts or thinking."

> From the disastrous consequence of a false *ism*, objectivism, we are in danger of collapsing into a false subjectivism where there are no criteria, but everything goes. Knowledge is neither purely objective nor purely subjective but is that which is available to the person who is personally and responsible committed to seeking the truth and publicly stating the findings.[5]

What is the place of reason in making ethical decisions? My "class of twenty-four" was asked, "How do you use reason to make ethical decisions?" A few comments from their small groups of four or five people follows.

- We found that reason is the tool to keep the other tools "honest" as we make ethical decisions.
- We use reason to prooftext our emotional responses. We use reason to discern whether our decisions are credible against the backdrop of emotions. Yet, belief and faith and heart often dictate our decisions in spite of what a rational, reasoning process may prescribe.

- Reason fleshes out the ethical expectations that critique irrational behavior.
- Reason leads to a definition of the problem, then looks at alternative solutions and possible consequences of each alternative.
- Reason helps us examine what the Bible, tradition, and community mores say about an issue. Praying about the issue may offer insight. Then we decide what to do.
- Reason itself is dictated by our experiences of the world; those things which impact our minds and influence our hearts. What is *reasonable* is determined, at least partially, by our cultures and communities.

Bruce C. Birch and Larry L. Rasmussen offer the following "Levels of Moral Discourse," which address reason in ethical decision making.

1. The first level is a simple expressive, or *emotive*, one. We straightforwardly register our feelings and judgments, without reflection or deliberation.

2. A second level is reached when a reflective dimension intrudes. We turn to ethical guides to help us reach a decision.

3. A third level is the justification for the decision. It asks why and on what grounds we answer the moral dimension of the "ought" question as we do, and it calls us to give public account of our working morality and its grounds.

4. A fourth level is identifying our *ultimate* loyalties and interest, our final beliefs and commitments. The authors believe "these convictions underlie the reasons given at the critical and reflective levels and usually ground the feelings at the emotive level."[6]

A Postscript to This Chapter

Albert Camus received the Nobel Prize in 1957. The presentation said:

Because, in everything he wrote, he spoke to us of our problems and, in our language, without raising his voice or indulging in oratory, he illuminated, as the Nobel citation stated, "the problems of the human conscience of our time." Over and above intellectual or political leadership, he provided the moral guidance the postwar [World War II] generation needed.[7]

Camus lived more than he believed; many people live less than they believe.

Questions for Reflection and Discussion

1. How do you use reason to make ethical decisions?

2. Remember an ethical issue you faced and examine how you used reason in making your decision. Did reason override emotions, or did emotions negate reason, or did both enjoy a complementary relationship?

3. Are you satisfied with the way your decision reflected your beliefs and values?

Notes

[1]Albert Camus, *The Stranger* (New York: Vintage Books, 1946).
[2]Albert Camus, *Resistance, Rebellion, and Death* (New York: Alfred A. Knopf, 1961), p. 73.
[3]Walter Truett Anderson, *Reality Isn't What It Used to Be* (San Francisco: Harper, 1990), p. 33.
[4]Darrell Jodock, *The Church's Bible* (Minneapolis: Augsburg/Fortress, 1984), p. 18.
[5]Leslie Newbigin, *Truth to Tell* (Grand Rapids: William B. Eerdmans Publishing Co., 1991), p. 21.
[6]Bruce C. Birch and Larry L. Rasmussen, *Bible and Ethics in the Christian Life* (Minneapolis: Augsburg/Fortress, 1989), pp. 112–113.
[7]Camus, *Resistance, Rebellion, and Death*, p. v.

9

Tradition: Frustrating Fact and Gracious Gift

When I was courting Catherine, I asked her for a date to go fishing the following Saturday. She accepted. Friday evening I prepared my fishing tackle; I oiled the Shakespeare reel, tested the line, and placed the reel on the new rod I had made.

On the way to Trout River in Jacksonville, Florida, we stopped at the fishing camp to purchase two dozen live shrimp. We arrived at my preferred fishing location about an hour before slack tide. Quickly unpacking the car, I rushed to my favorite spot on the wooden bridge, retrieved a shrimp from the bait can, slipped the hook through the shrimp's neck, and cast the tempter into the slow-moving waters. The float drifted just right. The weather was perfect; a cool breeze softened the sun's rays. I settled into my spot waiting for the float to disappear under the blue water.

Catherine stood by me in her cute white ruffled blouse, yellow shorts, and sandals. I fished. My eyes were staring at the float because exact timing was required to catch sea trout. From the time the float disappeared, you had to wait five seconds before yanking the pole—not two seconds or ten seconds. Yanking too soon pulled the shrimp out of the fish's mouth and too late the fish had lunch on you.

After about an hour, I glanced at Catherine and noticed that she did not seem to be having as much fun as I was; in fact, she looked pensive.

"What's wrong?" I asked.

She looked at me and said, "I didn't think we were *really* going to fish."

I apologized and told her I did not understand how we could have had this misunderstanding. She explained that for years, beginning when she was about five years old, her father took her fishing to the beach almost every Saturday. On Saturday morning, they grocery shopped for pork and beans, potted ham, wieners, sardines, crackers, cookies, candy, and other "nutritional" food. Then they drove to the jetties, where they had a trailer. Saturday and Sunday they played—wading and swimming in the ocean, holding hands while walking and skipping along the beach. They cooked and ate when they were hungry.

Ellis, Catherine's father, would say, "We're going fishing this weekend."

"So fishing for me," Catherine explained, "is wading in the water, holding hands, and playing with each other."

I reeled in my fishing line, released the shrimp, secured the hook to the rod, and took her hand as we walked back to the 1936 Ford convertible (old but beautiful). I put my fishing tackle in the car and we fished Catherine's way the rest of the day. For more than forty years we have had great fun fishing Catherine's way.

My experience of fishing also began when I was about five years old; my grandfather took me fishing. He taught me how to bait a hook and we fished, seldom saying more than "Pass the worms," "Nice catch," and "Let's eat." Our purpose for being at the river was to catch fish.

Though not a perfect illustration, the fishing incidents picture how we receive and live our traditions. Both Catherine and I had specific expectations of "fishing," with the rituals firmly fixed.

Loren	Catherine
Fishing tackle preparation alone; check tides	Grocery shopping with father
Catching fish	Playing with someone you love
Achievement (number of fish caught)	Relationships (time wading, swimming, walking, talking)
Competitiveness	Collaborativeness

After listening to Catherine's tradition, I agreed that her tradition was more fun than mine, at least for us.

Traditions shape our thoughts, feelings, and actions. Through tradition we know who we are, what is expected of us, what we are supposed to think, and how we are supposed to act ritually and ethically. Traditional rituals and rules often are assumed to be the way things ought to be.

> Tradition is the foundation of culture, a spiritual bond between the present and the past, between individuals and the greater fellowship in space and time, of which people are integrated members. What people know, their experiences and insights, what they have felt and thought and expressed in words, has, as far as it has been deemed important for the life and welfare of the community, been handed down by the tradition of mouth and documents and example.[1]

In religious circles it has become popular to say, "What is your source of authority? Is it experience, reason, tradition, or the Bible?" It reminds us of the sixties, seventies, and eighties cliché and icebreaker for dull people, "What is your sign?" The assumption was that the position of the stars at the moment of one's birth determined what kind of person you were supposed to be. In like measure, our traditions tell us who we are supposed to be. Tradition as our authority for ethical behavior influences who we are, how we are supposed to act, and what we can expect from others. It includes our position on holy scripture, basic beliefs about humankind (people are bad or people are good or...), and other fundamental values that give meaning to our lives.

The play *Fiddler on the Roof* opens with a man seated on the roof, playing a fiddle. A dairyman is outside the house looking at him.

A fiddler on the roof. Sounds crazy, no? But in our little village of Anatevka [Russia], you might say every one of us is a fiddler on a roof, trying to scratch out a pleasant, simple tune without breaking his neck. It isn't easy. You may ask, why do we stay up here if it's so dangerous? We stay because Anatevka is our home. And how do we keep our balance? That I can tell you in a word—tradition!

Because of our traditions, we've kept our balance for many, many years. Here in Anatevka we have traditions for everything—how to eat, how to sleep, how to wear clothes. For instance, we always keep our heads covered and always wear a little prayer shawl. This shows our constant devotion to God. You may ask, how did this tradition start? I'll tell you—I don't know! But it's tradition. Because of our traditions, everyone knows who he is and what God expects him to do.[2]

Traditions help us keep our balance in a postmodern, unstable world. There are positive and negative dimensions to tradition. As we examine these factors influencing our response to tradition, you, the reader, are encouraged to reflect on the traditions of the groups, institutions, and organizations that have given your life balance.

First, we will examine the positive dimensions of tradition.

1. Because tradition *feels* sacred, it gives us a sense of stability. We feel as if we are a part of something bigger than ourselves. Tradition feels right; God ordained it that way. Tradition offers emotional and spiritual stability.

2. Because of traditions, people know who they are. In a town where I served as pastor, people were identified by their church affiliation. John is a Baptist, Sue an Episcopalian, Allen a Church of Christ member, Mavis a member of the Christian Church, and Sarah is a Roman Catholic.

Jim said, "Mack looks like a Catholic." When I finished laughing I asked him how a Catholic looks.

Tradition transcends education, often perpetuates prejudice, and offers comfort to some people. Jim was a fine person with a master's degree from Harvard University, but he lived in a town where everyone was identified by his or her religious tradition.

Anderson addresses this issue when he observes that "We live in an age of the fading boundary, the twilight of a mind-set that structured reality with sharp lines. The boundaries between nations, classes, cultures, species—all become less distinct."[3] This fading boundary syndrome threatens people's emotional and spiritual identity; that is one reason some people reject any idea of the ecumenical movement in which church bodies (traditions) work together for the good of all humankind. Threatened people retreat to their church tradition where they can feel safe, secure, and superior.

3. Because of tradition, people *belong* to a community that is supposed to respect and care for them. The need for agency—a feeling of being in right relationships with others—offers people a sense of being important. They belong to something bigger than they are.

4. Because of tradition, people think they are making a contribution to their community, their ancestors, and their descendants. Their parents, grandparents, and other ancestors through the years, maybe centuries, have performed these rituals, lived by these traditional rules, and affirmed these same values.

5. Because of tradition, people know what God expects them to do; they know what is good and what is not. This sense of rightness affirms their sense of identity.

Second, we will examine the negative dimensions to tradition. Negative dimensions of tradition challenge our creativity and courage to affirm that which is worthy of loyalty and to eliminate that which is not.

"Don't sit on the bed," Virginia ordered her teenage son.

"Why?" Charles asked.

"Because you just don't sit on a bed after it is made up."

"But why?" argued Charles. "I like to study on the bed; it's more comfortable than the chair."

"Let's not talk about it. Just get off the bed."

"I could be out smoking pot, or robbing a convenience store, or stealing a car—and you get upset about my sitting on the bed."

Virginia thought for a minute and then confessed, "I don't know why you shouldn't sit on the bed after it's made up. My mother told me not to. I'll ask her."

Virginia's mother said, "My mother never let any of us kids sit on the bed after it was made. I think it was because we had feather mattresses and feather pillows, and if someone sat on the bed the feathers clumped and scattered and you had to start all over to make up the bed."

1. Traditional practices linger long after their rationale for being has dimmed in the memories of the members. People continue to believe and to practice their tradition but do not know why or how the practice came into being. Therefore tradition often loses its meaning for the next generation.

While the value of ritual and ethical standards gives some people emotional and spiritual stability, other people are untouched by these ideas and actions. The church's failure to interpret and evaluate the meaning and value of its rituals and rules often leaves the next generation on the outside. This exclusive "God has told us something that God has not told you" attitude performs an ethical/theological cleansing function, keeping the community pure for the remaining faithful.

The Orthodox Church is rich in tradition and knows how to keep it pure. Timothy Ware, Orthodox theologian and historian, explains.

> The thing that first strikes a stranger on encountering Orthodoxy is usually its air of antiquity, its apparent changelessness....Recently when two Orthodox scholars

were asked to summarize the distinctive characteristics of their church, they both pointed to the same things: its changelessness, its determination to remain loyal to the past, its sense of living continuity with the church of ancient times. Two and a half centuries before, the Eastern Patriarchs said exactly the same to the non-jurors: We preserve the Doctrine of the Lord uncorrupted and firmly adhere to the faith he delivered to us, and keep it free from blemish and diminution, as a royal treasure, and a monument of great price, neither adding any thing, nor taking any thing from it.[4]

The idea of living continuity is summed up for the Orthodox in the one word: tradition.

When questioned about the Orthodox Church's stand on prohibiting women from being ordained, the Greek Orthodox theologian explained that Jesus Christ is the Icon of God and since Jesus was a man, only men can be ordained. This theologian was not simply expressing a personal opinion, he was stating the Church's position that was established centuries ago.

"The Orthodox Christian of today sees *himself* as heir and guardian to a great inheritance received from the past, and *he* believes that it is *his* duty to transmit this inheritance unimpaired to the future," Ware explains (emphasis mine).[5]

Though not as structured, every religious group has tradition that is a protector of the truth. In a small, rural Christian Church (Disciples of Christ) congregation the church board was debating whether women could become elders. The men and some women were trying to keep the tradition of exclusion pure, when an eighty-five-year-old woman asked, "What does an inconspicuous appendage to the body have to do with spirituality?"

Because tradition tenaciously guards its identity and protects the status quo, when tradition contains unethical and harmful practices to outsiders and some inside the tradition, it perpetuates the practices in the name of tradition.

When church tradition, or any tradition for that matter, sustains sexism, reinforces racism, and ignores poverty and oppression while supporting a system in which women receive thirty percent less pay for the same work as men, and when it refuses to minister to AIDS victims, and accepts other abusive actions against people, the church violates the fundamental rationale for its existence. Of course, many people would disagree with the previous statement because of their tradition.

Questions for Reflection and Discussion

1. What criteria do we use to determine when to celebrate the tradition and when to exorcise the practice that is either meaningless or unjust to some people?

2. What does your tradition proclaim as its stances on major ethical issues of today?

3. Do you agree or disagree with those ethical positions? Why?

Notes

[1]*The Interpreter's Dictionary of the Bible*, George Arthur Buttrick, ed. (New York: Abingdon Press, 1902), pp. 683–685.

[2]Joseph Stein, *Fiddler on the Roof* (New York: Crown Publishers, Inc., 1964), pp. 2–3.

[3]Walter Truett Anderson, *Reality Isn't What It Used to Be* (San Francisco: Harper, 1990), p. 256.

[4]Timothy Ware, *The Orthodox Church* (New York: Penguin Books, 1963), pp. 203–204.

[5]*Ibid.*, p. 204.

10

The Bible as Ethical Authority

More than twenty years ago, Jeb Stuart Magruder (of Watergate infamy) stood before the judge and said, "Somewhere between my ambition and my ideals I lost my ethical compass." The *Reverend* Jeb Magruder has since recaptured that living guide; his ethical compass is the Bible. All Christians claim that their ethical compass is the Bible. Or do they?

Responses to the ethics survey item, "Briefly describe the way you make ethical decisions," did not confirm the above. Many people confessed that they do not know how they make ethical decisions and did not respond to that part of the questionnaire.

Five percent of laypeople surveyed made a direct reference to the Bible; 95 percent did not mention the Bible as a factor in their ethical life. Of the clergy, 32 percent referred to the Bible directly; 68 percent did not.

At least two circumstances surrounding the survey affected the responses. First, the people were not prepared in advance for the survey. They were asked to write their responses in specific settings: church school classes, family reunions, business seminars, youth retreats, and other sacred and secular settings. Second, the people were asked to respond in a limited amount of time; they were not given hours, days, or weeks to think about the "right" thing to write.

Though the Bible was not directly credited with giving guidance in making ethical decisions, its influence was evident in many cases. The following comments demonstrate such influence.

- Praying for and seeking the will of God.
- I ask what the faith tradition says.
- I make ethical decisions based on an awareness that Jesus Christ is the center of my life.
- Religion and faith. (?)
- I ask, "Is it the loving thing to do?"
- I weigh my humanness against the Christian ideal to which I feel called.
- I examine religious values and the effect the decisions will have on others.
- I ask, "What would Jesus do?"
- My decisions are with spiritual motivation. (?)
- I ask, "Will the decision please or displease God?"
- I use prayer and meditation.
- I use the church as the community of God to be the community of moral discernment.

Though some were influenced by the Bible, their response was so general as to be of little help in an ethical crisis. Others attempt to apply a specific biblical principle, e.g., "Do the loving thing." Still others use a biblical person, Jesus Christ, as a model for making decisions.

There were some who cited specific sayings as their ethical guide: "Do unto others as you would have them do unto you," "The Golden Rule," "Love your neighbor as yourself," and "The Ten Commandments." Most people in the survey did not demonstrate a holistic, systematic approach to the Bible for receiving ethical guidance; they evidently do not have a specific hermeneutic for discerning the truths contained therein.

It seems that most clergy and laity do not think about biblical authority as scholars do. In *Bible and Ethics in the Christian Life* the authors point out that "It is not at all clear how Bible and ethics are properly related. What is clear is that it is not a simple matter."[1]

The authority of the Bible in our lives and communities is a complicated issue and probably the most *practical* issue facing the church and society today. For when religious people discuss homosexuality, sexism in the church and society, abortion, capital punishment, ecological issues, poverty, oppression, and other ethical concerns, they usually arm themselves with biblical ideas, proof texts, and narratives to prove that God is on their side. Often these spiritual warriors use the Bible to defeat their enemies and exclude them from the inner circle of the "chosen ones," instead of stressing the inclusiveness of the gospel.

Though the subject is very complicated and requires volumes to do justice to it, the Bible as authority in making ethical decisions will be examined briefly. This is and should be taken on humbly, for I realize that God's existence and the authority of the Bible and the truths contained therein do not depend on my (or your) description of either.

In an interview Bill Moyers said, "Some movie stars think that if they had not been born, people would wonder why." Some Christians seem to think that if they do not prove to others that their approach to the Bible and understanding of scripture is the only true one, then the Bible will lose all its authority and God will become the equivalent of being dead. They believe that God depends on them to prove God's existence.

As we embark on this challenge let us remember what church historian Tertullian wrote: "Arguments about scripture achieve nothing but a stomachache or a headache."[2] While exploring this critical issue let us think together in a graceful spirit while attempting to identify how we perceive the Bible's authority and how it makes a difference in the way we treat our children, spouses, friends, coworkers, and neighbors.

As a child and teenager I attended Fairfield Christian Church in Jacksonville, Florida. Week after week I listened to the gentle Brother James White say such things as "Our loving God says that you are to believe in Jesus as Lord and accept him as your personal Savior or burn in hell forever," and "It is by God's grace that you are saved; and if you live a good, clean Christian life by not cursing, drinking alcohol, stealing, lying, and doing bad things, God will save you." (Bad things included having sex before marriage; though that was never said, it was understood. The "s" word was not used from the pulpit in the 1940s.)

Brother White did not see any contradiction between "God is love, and those who abide in love abide in God, and God abides in them" (1 John 4:16b) and "When I killed all the firstborn of Egypt, I consecrated for my own all the first-born of Israel, both human and animal, they shall be mine. I am the LORD" (Numbers 3:13b). Brother White's preaching was confusing to me—but evidently not to him. This saintly man believed that every word of the Bible was spoken by God, recorded by a faithful believer, and was true to the letter.

Since I am the firstborn I am glad that God did not choose to continue the practice of divine genocide. (The God I worship never did.)

Some biblical scholars still hold to Brother White's position of inerrancy of scripture. John O. Hosler explains:

> When contradictions seem apparent in the Bible, as in the case of Paul's faith without works and James' faith plus works, I must have confidence that God's true Word cannot be self-contradictory and that two contradictory positions cannot simultaneously be true. I know that I am in no position to choose which of the positions are of God. If the Bible is infallible and coherent in matters of faith and doctrine, then there is something that I am missing.[3]

Hosler has a static view of scriptures: the ideas, ideals, and *words* of the Bible are the foundation for faith. These words were written centuries ago and are as applicable to us today as they were the day they were written. According to this position, one must believe in the words of the Bible, even though they seem contradictory. It is one's lack of insight and understanding, not the texts of the Bible, that is the problem. One critic of this manuscript suggested that "this is not a bad place to begin."

Gloria Tate offers another approach. She believes that:

> Scriptures, rather than being the actual words of God, are testimonies and confessions of human beings as they understand God speaking to them. Inasmuch as these testimonies are based upon human experience and reflections on these experiences, they are subjective. This does not mean that they are inherently erroneous; however, subjectivity does create the environment for error. Nor can we dismiss the fact that the writings were handled by beings who were influenced by their history, social context, and worldview.[4]

> By saying that we must depend on "divine truth" as revealed in the Bible or else have no standards allows no room for the creative work of the Holy Spirit that generates revelation.[5]

Does this mean that Tate thinks and depends less on scripture than Hosler? By no means. Both search the scripture for truths by which to live and worship.

In his superb book *The Church's Bible*, Darrell Jodock offers the following understanding of the Bible.

> The scriptures are normative in their capacity to serve and mediate revelation, in their capacity to illumine and deepen the human experience of God's presence. They do not have a prescription for every problem, an answer to every question, or a blueprint for every future development. The church is not called to serve but to be served by the Bible.[6]

The Bible is God's gift to God's people. Our presuppositions caught early in life and our opinions about and beliefs in scripture certainly affect how we think we ought to live.

The New Testament scholar Sharyn Dowd has a simple, yet very helpful piece on "Attitude Toward the Bible." Identify yourself in the following.

A. If my attitude is like that of a *frightened slave or an abused child*, then I will approach the Bible as if it were a taskmaster or a parental authority.

- My questions will be: How can I stay out of trouble? What do I have to do to earn approval? It is a sin to....
- The result will be: I will find a list of rules, but God will become unnecessary. There is no need for God if all the questions are answered.

B. If my attitude is like that of a *rebel or lone ranger*, I will approach the Bible as if it were a boss or an external authority.

- My question will be: Why should I listen to any ideas except mine?
- The result will be that all I have to rely on is my own limited experience.

C. If my attitude is like that of a *trusted friend*, then I will approach the Bible as if it were a dialogue partner, a spiritual adviser, an acknowledged repository of wisdom and experience with God.

- My questions will be: Tell me what you know about God. Who is God? Who are we? What does it mean to be God's people? What do you mean when you say...?
- The result will be that I will learn what the biblical writers have to say. I will profit from their experiences of God, and come to know God for myself.[7]

Our attitude toward the Bible involves our experiences with parents, teachers, preachers, the church, and others. We catch attitudes from our environment: human, social, and institutional. That affects not only what we think about the Bible but how we feel about it. How *do* you feel about the Bible?

Questions for Reflection and Discussion

1. Using Dowd's "Attitude Toward the Bible," identify your approach to and use of the Bible in making ethical decisions.

2. Select a book of the Bible to apply this approach. Chapters 11 and 12 will aid you in this process.

Notes

[1]Bruce C. Birch and Larry L. Rasmussen, *Bible and Ethics in the Christian Life* (Minneapolis: Augsburg, 1989), p. 10.

[2]Quoted by David Scholer in *Conservative, Moderate, Liberal*, Charles R. Blaisdell, editor (St. Louis: CBP Press, 1990), p. 60.

[3]John O. Hosler in *Conservative, Moderate, Liberal*, p. 110.

[4]Gloria Tate in *Conservative, Moderate, Liberal*, p. 53.

[5]*Ibid.*, p. 50.

[6]Darrell Jodock, *The Church's Bible* (Minneapolis: Fortress Press, 1989), p. 120.

[7]Sharyn Dowd, unpublished outline. Used by permission.

11

The Bible as Proposition or Presence

In 1988, during the millennial celebration of the Russian Orthodox Church, Catherine and I joined tens of thousands of other American citizens who visited the Soviet Union. We worshiped almost daily in a Russian Orthodox church. We admired the grand architecture and art in St. Catherine's Cathedral and other church structures. We admired the babushkas (grandmothers) lighting candles, praying, and hushing whispering visitors. We stood in awe of the elaborate ritual. The churches were filled with people standing shoulder to shoulder every day for the two- or three-hour worship services. Communism could not crush the faithful.

At Leningrad Theological Seminary the New Testament professor spoke of the Christian and the Bible in the Soviet Union. When he came to the role of the Bible in the life of those oppressed people who paid dearly for practicing their faith, his voice rose a pitch higher, his eyelids narrowed, and his whole body braced itself as if going into battle.

"The Bible is liturgy. It is liturgy that gives people the strength to endure during difficult times. It is liturgy that holds the church together. It is liturgy that brings Christians together as the church."

This scholar paused, scanned the twenty-five faces looking at him, and as if the future of humankind depended on our understanding him and his message, he said, "Liturgy is

my hope. Liturgy is my life. Liturgy is everything." The Orthodox Church has a richer, deeper, more complex understanding and use of liturgy than most of us in Western
religions.

Yet this New Testament professor found in the Bible that
which he and others living in an oppressive society needed.
He and they needed worship. They needed to believe that,
contrary to the evidence, God was with them daily, and they
needed to know that other people were willing to sacrifice
for their faith too. They also needed a community of faith in
which they could tell and hear the stories of God's actions
with people, symbolically sharing their pains and problems,
fears and failures, and successes and victories. Every day the
liturgy told the story of God's redemptive action though Jesus
the Christ throughout history.

Our approach to and interpretation of scripture is always
contextual. That is, we see, select, understand, and accept
certain ideas and ideals in the Bible because of many
extrabiblical factors.

> All theories of biblical authority involve extrabiblical ap-
> peals to value or assumptions held by the prevailing
> culture....Prior to our reading of the scriptures, the images
> of God current in the community have influenced us.[1]

After accepting a call in 1964 to become the minister of
First Christian Church, Mayfield, Kentucky, I quickly learned
that there was a prevailing belief in the nature of God that
transcended the doctrinal differences between the people.
Though they were proud of their specific traditions (Southern Baptist, Episcopalian, Church of Christ, Presbyterian,
Disciples, etc.) in that community at that time, most people
agreed on the nature of God (good) and people (bad).

So prior to studying the scriptures they knew what they
would find out about God and people in the Bible, and sure
enough, they found what they expected to. Walter
Brueggemann explains:

We learned a certain perspective by living in certain contexts and listening to certain voices. Those might have been the voices of fearful parents or of calculating peers. They might have been the voices of grudging tradition or euphoric dreams.[2]

The ethics survey revealed just how strongly our parents' voices influence us. Our parents are influenced by the culture in which they lived and live. Remember: of the 2,192 do's and don'ts people listed, 1,661 were from parents, 230 from clergy, and 301 from grandparents, teachers, and others in our formative culture. Obviously these voices influence what we look for in scripture and how we interpret it.

What is taking place in our community and world at a particular time influences our approach to scripture. During World War II the lyrics of a popular song filled the radio airwaves: "Praise the Lord and pass the ammunition." George believes with all his heart that the "U.S. involvement in the war" was the will of God. With equal passion George said, "If everyone lived by the Ten Commandments the world's problems would be solved." "Thou shalt not kill?" The "Just War" theory was created to help us with our theological contradictions about killing people.

Brian Hebblethwaite reminds us that

In *The Cost of Discipleship*, Dietrich Bonhoeffer insists on obedience to the teaching of Jesus in the Sermon on the Mount, yet he did not believe that the command, "Resist not evil," could or should be applied directly to the state. And in his last years he came to believe it his Christian duty actively to support the plot to assassinate Hitler.[3]

"Honor your father and mother," when first written, was an appeal for the Israelite people to take care of their parents in old age and preserve the community. The commandment was given to discourage the practice of abandoning in the desert old, burdensome, irritating parents. Honoring parents made sense then as it does now for people who had and have loving, caring parents. But the victim of repeated sexual abuse by a father feels differently about honoring, respecting, and caring for that father when he gets too old to care for himself.

A Swedish pastor believes we must maintain the metaphor of God as Father, but reinterpret it. That would not be difficult if we and she were dealing with an intellectual idea. We are dealing primarily with nightmares, emotional trauma, permanent character scars, and constant fear for people repeatedly abused by their father or grandfather that affects how one understands the scripture.

Extrabiblical issues affect how we interpret the Bible and the ethical ideas/ideals we choose to believe and by which we hope to live. Barber von Wartenberg-Potter wrote:

> The Bible has a liberating message for women. This was what we discovered in a small workshop in India. We also became aware, however, that the Bible has often been used to reinforce negative cultural stereotypes about women, to denounce their struggle for equality, to discourage their full participation in church life and the ministries of the church. Embedded in a patriarchal culture and society, the early texts of the church often did not break through a value system which took men as the measure of humanity and women as secondary.[4]

Women in India probably will understand scripture differently than men on Wall Street. Peasants in Venezuela probably will not understand the Bible the same as the chief executive officer of a major corporation in the United States. (The Bible is still used in many cultures, social settings, and religious traditions to keep women oppressed.)

Living in the United States influences us greatly when it comes to approaches to the Bible. In the United States "individual rights" have been pulled to the top of the flagpole flying "Old Glory." Many people think and feel that their individual rights take precedence over everything else; that is what democracy is about, so they believe.

This radical individualism certainly affects how the Bible is interpreted, for the "worship" of the individual leads to narcissism, which makes "me" the center of the universe. The following satirical scene describes such thinking. An author says to a friend, "Let's talk about you. What do you think about my book?" Individualism turns everything inward. "My family exist to serve me." "My community exists for my benefit." "My church is there to meet my needs." "The Bible was written for my salvation and satisfaction." "God lives to bring me peace of mind."

The Bible exists for everyone's benefit. It is the book for the community of faith. The church attempts to break through the armor of narcissism to help people discover the values of living with and for others—narcissism is its own punishment, as the scriptures attest. Jesus' words point to this when he said, "Those who find their life will lose it, and those who lose their life for my sake will find it" (Matthew 10:39).

We need the community of faith to help us "lose our lives" in a cause bigger than our biblical narcissism. The community of faith interprets the scriptures; we help each other understand the meaning for our lives today. In a community of faith we:

1. Examine what tradition has to say about particular texts and issues. We listen to how others throughout history have interpreted the words. This communal act of remembering may save us from becoming victims of a Jim Jones or David Koresh type of cult or a "peace of mind" escapist.

2. Explore the context of the written words. Sharyn Dowd outlines this process as follows:

What the scriptural passage meant to the author and the audience in the first place.

   a. Who is speaking? Who is the audience? What are they like?

   b. How is the message communicated (story, poem, song, dialogue)?

    c. What is the content of the message?

    d. Why is the author saying this to these people?

    e. How does this fit with the rest of this document? With the rest of the writings of the author? With the rest of the Bible?

What it means to Christians today (reflection and prayer).

    a. How is the original audience like me/us?

    b. What does this say about how God wants to relate to me/us?

    c. What would it look like to respond obediently to this passage?

3. Listen to the stories of God's actions with and through Jesus and people; and

4. Discuss what this means for us as individuals living in a community of faith in a global village at this time.[5]

> The community of faith is the laboratory in which appropriate priorities are constructed and refined. A set of humane values is developed there to offer to the larger postmodern society, not by imposing them or even assuming that they are universally valid, but by modeling them and offering them freely. The church becomes one of several religions or ethically humanistic groups offering the larger society concrete embodiment of humane value, out of which a new ethical consensus may be fashioned.[6]

In community we encounter the Scriptures together and hopefully become people who live what we believe, even when that means disagreeing with each other over the Bible's positions on specific ethical issues. The spirit revealed in the Scriptures and embodied to some degree by the people of God holds us together in our and the Bible's diversity. Thereby we grow from our diversity (our differences) instead of growing apart because of them.

Jodock captures this thought when he writes:

Though the scripture should be understood and applied carefully, the ultimate goal of interpretation is not only to understand. Embodiment is the ultimate goal. The Scriptures mediate the presence of God, an arresting, transforming, identity-forming, and relationship-forming presence. An encounter with the presence of God calls for an existential response to be embodied in a renewed life that lives the shalom of God's kingdom."[7]

The Bible contains a universal truth that is valid for all people in all times in all cultures. There is a basic ethic given through the Bible for all people in a postmodern, pluralistic world. It is to that that we now turn by giving a brief exposition of Romans with emphasis on Romans 12, which is St. Paul's basic ethical mandate.

As you read Romans do so with two attitudes. First, read Romans with the critical mind seeking to discover exactly what the words and ideas mean. Use Dowd's approach. Second, suspend the critical mind and read Romans primarily listening to what the scriptures are saying and experience the emotional and spiritual depth of the messages.

Notes

[1]Darrell Jodock, *The Church's Bible* (Minneapolis: Fortress Press, 1989), pp. 71, 91.

[2]Walter Brueggemann, *The Bible Makes Sense* (Atlanta: John Knox Press, 1985), p. 9.

[3]Brian Hebblethwaite, *Christian Ethics in the Modern Age* (Philadelphia: The Westminster Press, 1982), p. 95.

[4]Barber von Wartenberg-Potter, *By Our Lives* (Geneva: The World Council of Churches, 1985), p. vii.

[5]Sharyn Dowd, unpublished paper.

[6]Jodock, p. 83.

[7]*Ibid.*, p. 143.

12

A Transforming Book: Romans 12

God's Actions—Romans 1–11

St. Paul is not an ordinary saint; that is, if we mean by *saint* someone who is radically different from ordinary people. Paul was a compulsive, argumentative, and sometimes arrogant person. Therefore, there were Christians who not only disliked him, but did not trust him. Karl Barth explained, "This controversial and argumentative man intended to travel to Rome, and he therefore considered it necessary and right to introduce himself to the Christians there."[1] Instead of riding into Rome on his shaky reputation (at least according to some of Paul's critics), Paul wanted these people, whom he probably did not know, to get their opinion of Paul from the primary source—Paul himself.

So Paul wrote a letter that has had a profound effect upon Christians in every generation. Romans is Paul's theology in its most complete form. It is both a personal message addressed to individuals and a theological treatise addressed to the church in all ages. Romans contains a code of ethics that is applicable to all people in all ages.

We can identify with Paul because his words are so contemporary. "I do not understand my own actions," Paul confesses. "For I do not do what I want, but I do the very thing I hate" (Romans 7:15). We can identify with this experience of not living up to our ideals, if not always in fact, then certainly in fantasy: our fantasies of fun born out of a boring, routine life; fantasies of revenge emerging out of resentments caused by personal hurts; fantasies of righteousness and heroic deeds compensating for feelings of spiritual and emotional impotency. We can identify with Paul.

Paul Achtemeier describes the relevance of Romans.

> Paul deals with problems as global as the headlines and as intimate as those described in "Dear Abby." The fate and future of the Jewish people, the role of the individual in the total sweep of history, the responsibilities of the citizens to the government of the country with which he or she may not agree, the morality of actions in which adults engage, sexual and otherwise. All these and more occupy Paul in his letter to the Christians in Rome."[2]

Romans has had a profound effect upon individuals who helped to shape the Christian tradition. St. Augustine, Martin Luther, and John Wesley credited Romans for some form of personal spiritual transformation of their lives. John Calvin wrote, "When someone gains a knowledge of this epistle he has an entrance opened to him to all the most hidden treasures of Scripture."[3]

Paul's theology, his beliefs, grew out of his personal *experience* of God as revealed through Jesus Christ. So he is writing about who he has been, what happened to him spiritually, therefore who he is now, and what the future will be for all people. Remember: Romans is primarily a "confession" based on God's presence in Paul's life.

The reason Paul wrote to the Christians in Rome is twofold. First, he wanted to visit the Christians in Rome (who were well known to other church people) to speak (preach) to them and to hear from them accounts of their experiences of the Christian faith; and second, Paul needed a stopover place on his way to Spain to continue his missionary work to the Gentiles. Before the journey to Rome and Spain, Paul has to take money given by Gentile Christians to the church in Jerusalem. This money is probably a peace offering not only to help financially, but to try to improve relations between Jews and Gentiles—between "conservative" Christians and "liberal" Christians. How contemporary can Romans be? People on both sides of this theological/sociological/psychological debate could benefit from a study of Romans.

The message of Romans is about the past, what has happened between God and people before Jesus Christ, what happened and is happening with and through the spirit of Jesus Christ, and what the future holds for all people.

Paul Achtemeier outlines three themes in Romans. The past is represented by Adam (old eon) in which disobedience to God (sin) prevailed and dominated people and groups of people (Israel). The results of this rebellion are spiritual and physical death. No matter how hard people tried to be righteous by following the law (laws) of God, they failed.

Through the coming of Christ the present age was ushered into history. The Spirit of God was (is) experienced by people. After the presence of God enters one's life, obedience is possible because people are reconciled to God through their experience of God's Spirit. "For if while we were enemies, we were reconciled to God through the death of his Son, much more surely, having been reconciled, will we be saved by his life. But more than that, we even boast in God through our Lord Jesus Christ, through whom we have now received reconciliation" (5:10–11).

The future promises the new eon, which has already begun God's visible rule and salvation for all people. Our hopes, dreams, and beliefs about the future are certainly a part of who we are today, as were Paul's beliefs about the future for him.

In the old eon before Christ, people lived narcissistically; they believed they controlled their destiny. God gave them the Law (laws of living); they used the Law to try to prove their worth and to justify their behavior. People believed they could live up to the Law with their willpower. This reflected a faith in oneself, not God. Trying to keep the Law was just another form of narcissism—self-worship. (How contemporary can Paul be?)

Martha, fifty-eight years old, was a member of her women's church group. She never missed a group meeting at which she proudly proclaimed her hospital visits to sick people. Martha could hardly wait for a friend or acquaintance or a friend's acquaintance to be hospitalized.

On such occasions, Martha armed herself with stories of other people's illnesses and an autobiography of her struggles with sickness, then stalked into the hospital room and assaulted the defenseless patients with details of disease and death. She reminds one of Philip Roth's description of his father's behavior as "hock." Roth defined "hock" as a yiddishism that in this context means to badger, to bludgeon, to hammer with warnings and edicts and pleas—in short, "to drive a hole in somebody's head with words."[4]

Martha "hocked" patients and left them exhausted and depressed while she emotionally skipped from one hospital room to another, checking her list, being a good Christian by "visiting the sick."

The "law" of visiting the sick can be a helpful religious act. But because Martha is living in the old eon—in sin—she abuses the law because she is still bound to thinking primarily about herself; she calls on sick people for Martha's sake. Calling on sick people causes her to feel altruistic, religious, pious. Martha is not visiting the sick for their well-being, although she thinks she is.

Paul declared that there is not anything wrong with the law before or after Christ. "What then should we say? That the law is sin? By no means!...For we know that the law is spiritual....There is therefore now no condemnation for those who are in Christ Jesus. For the law of the Spirit of life in Christ Jesus has set you free from the law of sin and of death" (7:7, 7:14, 8:1–2).

The first eleven chapters of Romans describe what God has done for us. God's grace transforms us. The presence of God is in our midst. Achtemeier explains:

> Righteousness by faith [not works] is the means by which God's gracious lordship may now be accepted by all, whether Jew or Gentile, and hence is the means by which Paul understands the gospel to be universal in extent. Righteousness by faith is also the way God makes the ungodly righteous (4:5). Yet, as such, it is subordinated to the larger point that such righteousness is now open to all who follow Abraham in trusting God to do what [God] has promised, namely, to make Abraham a blessing to all people.[5]

Abraham lived by faith in God and not in his own ability to be righteous and act righteously without God.

Our Responses to God—Romans 12

In "Adam's reign" people believed they could earn their salvation, their sense of spiritual well-being, their righteousness, their spiritual serenity. These people thought they were loved because they were worthy; that is, they thought if they could act properly and score enough ritual and righteous points they would please God and be loved.

Paul proclaims the opposite. We are worthy because we are loved. The tension between doing the "law" to get a sense of worth and accepting in faith the grace of God resides in us.

Our sense of personal meaning in life is always linked with our sense of personal worth. And our feelings of worth are affected by parents, friends, communities, and God. We are worthy because we are loved by God—that's Paul's conviction. Yet we need people to affirm that sense of worth with their love. Thus we need community. "Love one another with mutual affection" (12:9).

Because of God's love for us and God's presence in us and between us and others in community, we are to be transformed by the renewing of our minds so that we may discern what the will of God is—"what is good and acceptable and perfect" (12:2). God's presence changes the way we think about, feel for, and perceive people, events, and institutions. Action follows being. The experience precedes the ethical behavior. Our actions are a result of who we have become because of God's presence in us.

With such an experience, instead of standing as erect as a Marine at attention when she "hocks" patients in the hospital, Martha may sit in a chair by the bed and listen to her friend, Betty, talk about her illness, family, fears, and hopes.

Romans 12 begins Paul's ethical instructions for those who have experienced the Spirit of Christ. A brief overview follows.

1. We belong together in community; we are "members one of another." We are interdependent people who share our love and gifts.

2. Every person is respected and honored with her or his gift.

3. With enthusiasm, respect, and joy we contribute to the saints and welcome strangers. Ideally we care for all people, not just those inside the church.

4. With patience and prayer we empathize with people, even our critics and persecutors.

5. We refuse to be overcome with evil; we overcome evil with good.

6. As far as possible we create a community of people who live peaceably—a community characterized by trust, mutual respect, humility, joy, patience, faith, and love.

Paul is describing the ideal ethical theme of the New Testament. Obviously, to be able to come close to living this ideal we need help; in fact, we need to affirm and accept that God through and with us can create such characters and communities.

Paul also recognizes the conflict between the ideal and the real for those who have experienced God's presence. His ethical ideas/ideals applied to us in the twentieth century might read as follows.

1. Though we may have an experience of God's presence as Abraham, Jesus, Gandhi, and Martin Luther King, Jr. did, we need guidance to try to live the implications of the experience.

2. Even with the experience and ethical instructions, we still have difficulty living the ideal. The reason is that we cannot erase our past. The old self continues to contaminate our good intentions. Our narcissism is not easily erased. Our past is always a part of who we are today.

3. Because of the above, we need others to help us live ethically as we struggle with sickness, sin, and sadness as well as success, self-satisfaction, and pseudo-serenity. We need people who care about us to confront us when we are calloused to the hurt of others and to comfort us when we fail or feel hopeless and worthless, and to cheer us when we occasionally perform altruistically.

4. We certainly need God and others to help us overcome the old self's need to "punch out" the energy.

Paul is urging us to trust God and to co-create with God a community of people who sometimes will act altruistically toward others, including welcoming the stranger. There is much more to Romans. Read it and risk being transformed spiritually and emotionally.[6]

Interlude: the Authority of "Presence"

Though we need some system to guide us in making ethical decisions in a postmodern world, we need more than manageable methods for making difficult decisions.

From Romans we learn that we need an experience of God, an experience of transformation, to empower us to act altruistically—to want to see and do the truth. One change that occurred during the Enlightenment was, according to Langdon Gilkey, "A renewed emphasis on love rather than on purity of faith." In the *Institutes* Calvin held that the latter requirement took precedence over loving one's neighbor.[7]

What you believed counted more than what you did. That battle continues. There are those who find it much easier to believe right than to do right, and thereby "feel" self-righteous.

I am reminded again of Lorrie Moore's words in writing about emotionally cold people: "For them it is all honesty before kindness."[8] Yet, honesty is also essential in the search for truth.

When Mark, Tammy, Army, and Alisha moved into their "new" home, the previous owners had left a saying on their refrigerator, which captures some of our thought.

> Without honesty there is no truth,
> Without truth their is no understanding,
> Without understanding there is no love,
> Without love there is nothing.

To live altruistically, then, we need both an individual experience and a community in which we are encouraged and affirmed as we try to live what we believe, because we never completely arrive ethically. We are always in process of becoming who we and God would have us become or we are fighting the lure of God. In this evolving process, though it does not guarantee that we will always try to do the loving thing, even if you know it, the empowering presence of God increases the probability of our caring about and acting to help others in their quest for a more humane way of life. Humankind depends on such people of goodwill for survival.

Questions for Reflection and Discussion

1. Identify the virtues Paul records in Romans.

2. Compare Paul's virtues with the virtues you listed.

3. Does Paul believe in an "absolute" (universally valid) ethic? If so, describe it.

Notes

[1]Karl Barth, *A Shorter Commentary on Romans* (Richmond: John Knox Press, 1989), p. 11.

[2]Paul Achtemeier, *Romans* (Atlanta: John Knox Press, 1985), p. 1.

[3]D. Stuart Briscoe, *The Communicator's Commentary: Romans* (Waco: Word Books, 1982), p. 12.

[4]Philip Roth, *Patrimony* (New York: A Touchtone Book, 1991), p. 80.

[5]Achtemeier, p. 21.

[6]The following books give a balanced approach to the study of Romans and Paul's theology as well as those already noted.

William Barclay, *The Mind of Paul* (New York: Harper, 1958).

Emil Brunner, *The Letter to the Romans* (Philadelphia: Westminster Press, 1959).

Brendan Byrne, S.J. and Michael Glazier, *Reckoning with Romans* (Wilmington: Michael Glazier, 1986).

C.E.B. Cranfield, *Romans* (Grand Rapids: William B. Eerdmans, 1985).

Anders Nygren, *Commentary on Romans*, tr. Carl C. Rasmussen (Philadelphia: Muhlenberg Press, 1949).

For brief articles on Roman culture and on Paul's letter to the Romans, see: *The Interpreter's Dictionary of the Bible*, Vol. R–Z. Editor: George Arthur Buttrick (New York: Abingdon Press, 1962).

In *The Bible Today*, Vol. 32:2 (March 1993), Mary Ann Getty has an interesting article entitled "Sin and Salvation in Romans," pp. 89–93.

[7]Langdon Gilkey, *Through the Tempest* (Minneapolis: Augsburg Fortress, 1991), p. 22.

[8]Lorrie Moore, *Self-Help* (New York: Harper and Row, 1965), p. 36.

13

The Presence

After several tests, Dr. James Orr said, "It's not a heart attack, Loren. You had a severe angina attack; we will treat it with rest and medication." (1975 was an interesting year.) I dozed off in the hospital room; the other bed was unoccupied when I went to sleep.

Upon awakening the next morning, I stared at the stranger in the other bed. Lying on his side, facing away from me, was an anemic-looking elderly man. During the first hour of the new day, he groaned while sleeping, which caused me to speculate about the problems a sick roommate can cause one. I did not want a seriously ill person in the same room with me in the hospital. A very healthy, lively, interesting person ought to be renting the bed.

Later in the morning, while still half-asleep, he rolled to face the window—and me. He resembled someone I knew. Gradually he awakened, and we began to chitchat about everything from voyeurs designing hospital gowns to the time of our next meal. After a few hours of visiting I figured out whom he looked like. His high cheekbones, slim five-foot-seven-inch body, and brownish gray hair reminded me of an eighty-five-year-old Woody Allen. During the next two days I discovered that this weak body contained the emotional power of a Mahatma Gandhi and the spiritual strength of a St. Francis of Assisi.

Mr. Halneck was a Russian-born Jew who lived his first twenty years in Russia. Born in 1890, he experienced the turbulent years of the Bolshevik Revolution. At the age of ten he attended secret meetings to learn about the upcoming revolution. The meetings were held on sight-seeing boats. The young students stood side by side, viewing the countryside, while a teacher quietly talked to them of the new Russia that would come to be, someday.

Mr. Halneck was shy in a special way. He was reluctant to talk about himself; it took some prodding to get him to share some of his early life experiences. Gentle persistence paid off.

When he was twenty years old, Mr. Halneck was forced to join the army. He was told that if he did not enter the army his mother's property would be confiscated. Because he did not believe in the cause of the ruling regime, he could not, in good conscience, fight for the army against the underdog peasants. Fortunately for Mr. Halneck, the army was "corrupt," and it took but a relatively small fee to arrange for his release from military service. Shortly thereafter, he escaped to America. Sixty-five years later he was still dreaming of a free new Russia. When he talked of this dream, his eyes flashed, his hands darted about, and he sat erect in his hospital bed. He loved the homeland as it could be, not as it was.

During his years in Russia, Mr. Halneck felt the sting of anti-Semitism. What Mr. Halneck alluded to, George Von Rauch described in *A History of Soviet Russia*. "Unrest among the masses was increased by anti-Jewish programs [which, beginning in October, 1905] rolled like a wave over western and southern Russia."[1] The fifteen-year-old boy felt the pestilence of prejudice intensify as he entered his adolescent years. This irrational disease, which destroys so many people, was not new to him. After many hours of sharing our lives together, Mr. Halneck told a touching story.

He was nine years old; his father was dead. On the day of the "event" he, his mother, and his brother busied themselves placing silverware, china, favored murals, special objects, family pictures, and some furniture in their small basement. The entrance to the basement was concealed from the casual visitor. After the task was finished, they waited and tried to fill the time with small talk and stories of the past.

About nine o'clock at night, the dreaded noise echoed in the distance. Mrs. Halneck called her two young sons to her side on the deacon's bench. The loud voices came closer and closer to the home. When the voices sounded as though they were at the front door, Mrs. Halneck put her arms around her two sons, pulled them to her bosom, hunching partially over them, while they waited on the hard bench for their fate. The voices ceased singing "Onward Christian Soldiers." It was Palm Sunday. The "Christians" were celebrating their savior's entry into Jerusalem in their usual way. A description of that ritual follows.

Voices mumbled outside the door. Crash! The front door flew open and in rushed men, women, and children swinging palm leaves tied together in heavy bunches. Several people charged toward the young boy, his mother, and his brother; they started beating them with their palm leaves. Other "Christians" smashed mirrors, broke windows, and destroyed furniture. Stoically Mrs. Halneck tried to protect her children. No bones were broken, but skin was slashed and blood oozed from the wounds. Dark blue-purple bruises later appeared where the "Christians'" Palm Sunday symbols had torn tissue inside the skin covering the backs, arms, legs, and faces of the simple Jewish family members.

At nine years of age, Mr. Halneck could not conceive a reason why these people wanted to hurt him, his mother, and his brother, or why they destroyed the Halnecks' property. The Halnecks were responsible citizens in the town, did not intentionally offend anyone, and did not criticize others' religions. Mr. Halneck's mother could not explain it to him. To add to the confusion of a nine-year-old boy, on Monday following Palm Sunday, everyone pretended as though nothing unusual had happened the night before at the Halnecks' home. There was no talk about it, no apologies, no additional cursing or beating or destroying; the riotous ritual had run its course. Some people acted as though that event had been erased from history; yet it can never be erased from the memory and heart of a holy man named Halneck.

While Mr. Halneck calmly described this incident, I became angrier and angrier. In my heart I wanted to do to the "Palm Sunday priests" what they did to the Halnecks, thus reflecting the spirit of the pious palmists rather than that of the hallowed holy man.

Mr. Halneck was a gift of grace. He was a delightful person, a deep thinker who philosophized occasionally about world political systems, religious concepts, and people. The mellowness of the man was an invisible mural of meaning; it was something one *felt* in his presence. With every reason imaginable to hate, he intoned forgiveness. Forgiveness was not an act he performed; it was a quality of feeling communicated to all who ventured into his presence. Acceptance was not behavioral-science jargon or religious rhetoric for Mr. Halneck; it was a way of life that affirmed others. He had ideals that he expounded upon with eloquence. Yet the individual, that special unit of creation in the flesh, was always accepted as presented. Mr. Halneck did not yield to the temptation to be prejudiced; it seemed that anyone who entered his life was accepted as a special act of creation itself. Refusing to believe generalizations about people, he related to each speck of creation as something sacred. He perceived people as individuals without letting role labels blur his vision of reality or corrupt his spirit of compassion.

Jesus did not come to establish an exclusive club but to create an inclusive community through which the presence of God could be communicated. Mr. Halneck embodied that Presence.

The absolute ethic is not a specific proposition or principle but a Presence. It is a Presence, an idea/ideal, that addresses the postmodern, pluralistic age because it is not confined to any one ideology or theology. "People at the edge [in crisis] need a presence, not a preacher."[2] That Presence is not limited by my or your experience, tradition, or biblical hermeneutic. Mr. Halneck embodied the Presence that my religious tradition professes and confesses.

The Christian faith proclaims that God through Jesus Christ offers a Presence that will be with us always. "And remember, I am with you always, to the end of the age." (Matthew 28:20). The Holy Spirit, the Spirit of God, and the Spirit of Christ are interchangeable concepts, all reflecting the Christian's description of the Presence.

My past, present, and future are encompassed in the Christian faith and traditions. My primary authority for living is the Bible, understood and interpreted through my tradition, experience, and reasoning. As naive as it may appear, my primary conviction, my fundamental belief about creation, is that "God is love and those who abide in love abide in God, and God abides in them" (1 John 4:16). Where God is, love is; where love is, God is. That love is the Presence that makes a difference in us and between us and others.

The absolute ethic, then, is not a preposition or a principle, but a Presence that is embodied in and manifested through people.

What was it about Simone Weil that caused T.S. Eliot, André Gide, Albert Camus, and others to praise her "saintly" life? It was a Presence, a quality of character, that motivated her to try to do the loving thing, and which transcended her masochistic mania. She was not perfect; T.S. Eliot described her as a "difficult, violent and complex personality, yet one who might have become a saint."[3]

The specialness of Gandhi, Martin Luther King, Jr., St. Paul, Jesus, the nurse Betty, Mr. Halneck, and many others, is not their morally superior stance or high intelligence, but a Presence indwelling them that motivated them to try to do the loving thing. Somehow these people transcended their narcissistic need for personal safety, self-satisfaction, and security to try to ease the pain of others and to help develop a more just and humane society. Millions of other people believed and quietly lived and live the words of Nicolas Berdyaev: "Bread for myself is a natural concern, bread for my neighbor is a spiritual concern."[4]

To be concerned for and act on behalf of one's neighbor is a manifestation of the Presence in people and institutions. It is a spiritual and ethical quality of character. Some of the people described herein will be models of the Presence and reflect the character in return, because the Presence is also a process of becoming who we were created to be.

Writing about emotionally cold people, Lorrie Moore explained, "They never learn the beauty or value of gesture, the emotional necessity. For them, it is all honesty before kindness, truth before art. Love is art, not truth. It's like painting scenery."[5]

Lorrie Moore was half-correct—love is art *and* truth. The truth and art of the Presence that creates character addresses the challenge Darrell Jodock presents when he wrote:

> The task in the postmodern age is not to turn back the clock or impose limits on freedom but to find some authentic sense of transcendence that will guide the experience of human freedom and prevent its destructive excesses.[6]

Questions for Reflection and Discussion

1. When reading about Mr. Halneck, whom do you think about?

2. What was special about that person? Try to describe what made the person special.

3. Were you somehow different in the presence of this person than you are at other times with other people?

Notes

[1]George Von Rauch, *A History of Soviet Russia,* translated by Peter and Annette Jacobson (New York: Frederick A. Praeger, 1957), p. 23.

[2]David P. Polk, ed., *What's a Christian to Do?* (St. Louis: Chalice Press, 1991), p. 59.

[3]William O. Paulsell, *Tough Minds, Tender Hearts* (New York: Paulist Press, 1990), p. 30.

[4]Michael Kinnamon contributed this quote in his critique of the manuscript.

[5]Lorrie Moore, *Self-Help* (New York: New American Library, 1985), p. 39.

[6]Darrell Jodock, *The Church's Bible* (Minneapolis: Fortress Press, 1989), p. 77.

14

Living Stories—Thinking Lives

Betty Colter Collins was taking a course at Lexington Theological Seminary entitled "Stewardship: A Way of Life." She read the eight books required and demonstrated a knowledge of the theological, psychological, and biblical material.

The final paper assignment was to write her theology in which she was to give the authority for her beliefs—where did she learn what she believed? Instead of preparing the expected academic paper littered with quotes and endnotes from wise scholars, she wrote the following.

> "Stewardship—A Way of Living" has deep-rooted implications for me. My earliest memories of stewardship in action come from childhood. My mother truly lives the ideal of a good steward. Through her, I learned to appreciate my obligation to people. Through her, I learned to share with others what was entrusted to me. Through her, I learned to love one another, even when others were not loving in return. Through her, I learned not to be judgmental, to look for good in all people, and to have a forgiving heart. Through her, I learned to appreciate what the earth had to give, and to give back to the earth. My mother is a good steward. She taught her children through living example what it means to live a Christian life.

My early lesson on stewardship had to do with living in a large poor family. Being one of nine children, living in rural Boyle County, poor, and black, offered numerous opportunities to witness true stewardship. Mother would say, "Be thankful for what we have, many have less." She made our house a happy home. Though we had little, especially by today's standards, we were blessed. Our blessings were in a form of happiness, health, companionship, and love. To me, that's good stewardship, giving thanks and being glad with what you had, even when times are hard.

Mother taught us to look beyond ourselves to others who were in need. Though poor, we shared food with neighbors who had no food. Mother would say, "If I have a slice of bread, and my neighbor has none, then I must give half." Over and over again I witnessed my mother sharing whatever we had with less fortunate souls. Mother truly believes it is her Christian duty to help others, and to look for others who might need help.

Again, mother taught us to love one another and to be kind to each other and to be loving toward our neighbors and to treat all people with respect. This lesson was a tough one for us to grasp, but Mother persisted. Finally, I understand the true implications of this concept. Mother knew that we as siblings would not always be loving to one another and that as poor blacks we would face many who despised and hated us, yet she said God still expects us to love one another. A loving spirit can break down walls of hate. This lesson has brought me through many tough times when I was surrounded by people who judged me by standards other than my merits.

Mother taught us to look for good in people and to build on that good. This taught me that each of us has good and bad qualities; that we should not expect perfection in others when we ourselves are not perfect. From this I learned humility. Therefore no matter how great I may think I am at a particular time in a particular area of life, I am not perfect. This concept helps me to accept others as they are and to try to build the foundation of trust and love with them.

Mother made maximal usage of the earth and its many gifts. When I was a child, we farmed, picked, and hunted for the food God provided. We were never hungry and never wanted for the necessities of life. Mother used her many talents to feed us and others. Yet, she preserved the land, taking care not to disrupt nature.

My mother, though uneducated and poor, knew God's grace and blessings. She is a remarkable person and truly lives the life of a good steward.

The numerous lessons learned at my mother's side have followed me into my adult life, as I try to live the life of a good steward. I have been blessed with opportunities to help others in need, both professionally and personally.

I am a nurse by profession. This profession affords me numerous opportunities in which to practice stewardship. God blessed me with a caring heart, which allows me to offer comfort and support to families and patients facing illness, pain, and death. Caring for others provides me with great satisfaction. For this I am thankful.

God has also blessed me with many opportunities to be a good steward in my personal life. I have shared my home with homeless families. This sharing met the needs of the families and gave me pleasure, as well as lifelong friendships. For those opportunities I am thankful and blessed.

For me, "stewardship—a way of life" means opening our hearts and minds to the needs of others. It means using our time, talent, and money to spread God's good news. It means recognizing that all we have belongs to God and is entrusted in us to use to do God's will.[1]

Betty's story shows us how people with the presence of God live. Their values, emotions, and behavior reflect the absolute ethic. These people welcome the stranger in a radical way. The stranger is greeted, invited into the home, accepted by the family, affirmed as worthy and equal companions, and made into a friend. "For I was hungry and you gave me food, I was thirsty and you gave me something to drink, I was a stranger and you welcomed me" (Matthew 25:35).

People live stories; they do not think lives into being in a logical, systematic way. If we want to know who we are and what we value and the moral quality of our lives, we tell our stories. As Betty did, we describe events, people, feelings, and thoughts. If we want to know who others are we listen carefully to the stories they tell and "pay attention" to how they live. This in no way diminishes the importance of ethics—the ideas/ideals of living.

Betty demonstrates one of the ideas Robert Coles stresses in his excellent book *The Call of Stories*. Coles emphasizes that stories (ours, as well as those of others and fictional characters) have a way of connecting our intellectual experiences—the seemingly abstract ideas—with our everyday living experiences.[2] Reading Betty's paper sent me in search of Coles' concept because she integrated ideas about life with her past experiences and present living.

Coles also had a similar experience that sent him back to a passage from *The Brothers Karamazov*. Alyosha addressed the young people who admired him.

My children…you must know that there is nothing higher and stronger and more wholesome and good for life in the future than some good memory, especially a memory of childhood, of home. People talk to you a great deal about your education, but some good sacred memory, preserved from childhood, is perhaps the best education. If one carries such memories into life, one is safe to the end of one's days, and if one has only one good memory left in one's heart, even that may be the means of saving us.[3]

Experiencing an idea, a memory, a concept, a theory, is called *praxis*. Praxis is where theory—thinking—intersects with practical living. Parents give us memories and most memories have ethical assumptions in them—a right way to live according to their values. So when a memory emerges from our past in the form of a special event or specific idea/ideal, it tests our living.

Janice was having an affair. Janice's spouse suspected she was having the affair, but could not prove it. That did not stop him from fighting with Janice over the possibility. In a conference she blurted out,"Reverend Broadus, he's impossible to live with. He makes me so mad…he's so critical. I'm tired of his accusing me of all the things I do."

Many who responded to the questionnaire felt the sting of not living up to their parents' ethical standards or/and resented the memory of such standards; they were convicted by the memory accusing them of what they were doing.

Others discussed their memories of parents' ethical expectations with a sense of nostalgia and appreciation of what they had been taught even though some of these people rejected the specific do's and don'ts. "If one carries such memories into life, one is safe to the end of one's days, and if one has only one memory left in one's heart, even that may be the means of saving us."

Some people have become friends with the memories their parents created with them and use these memories as a barometer of their moral and spiritual growth, or the lack of it.

They may laugh at the naive assumptions of some sayings for today's world while still appreciating the reasons their parents said such things. These people know their parents loved them. Some other people are not so lucky.

It might be helpful to write or tell your story, as Betty did.

Questions for Reflection and Discussion

1. Try to identify the characteristics of an ethic of presence in Betty's story.

2. Are these characteristics prevalent in the lives of the people nearest to you? In you?

Notes

[1] Used by permission.

[2] Robert Coles, *The Call of Stories* (Boston: Houghton Mifflin Company, 1989), p. 183.

[3] *Ibid.*, p. 193.

15

Welcome the Stranger

The temptation and tendency of Christians is to define so rigidly their specific church tradition with its ritual, rules, and rightness that it excludes all others from the saving grace of God. *"Only* by accepting Jesus as Lord and Savior and by believing our doctrines will you be saved," Martha proudly proclaims. Martha feels sorry for people who have not seen "the true light of the Lord's blessing," because she knows that she and her church are God's pets, chosen people, and the only chosen people.

Martha and Goethe have something in common. Kundera wrote that Goethe "considered himself the administrator of his immortality, and that responsibility tied him down and turned him stiff and prim."[1] Martha is not only the administrator of her immortality, but the distributor of God's grace. She decides who is in and who is out.

John considers himself a religious liberal because he thinks that even some Southern Baptists, Roman Catholics, and others with doctrinally deficient traditions may be saved by God's grace, in spite of their flawed faith. He also believes that *only* those who say the magical words "I accept Jesus as my Lord and Savior" will be accepted by God. This confession of faith is the key to the Kingdom.

In contrast to these positions, Darrell J. Fasching believes that "the good news is not some ideology to be imposed on others but the eschatalogical event that occurs when we welcome the stranger. We do not bring Christ to the stranger. We meet Christ in the stranger."[2]

We experience the presence of God in the stranger when we feed the hungry, give a drink of water to the thirsty, clothe the naked, take care of the sick, visit those in prison—"Just as you did it to one of the least of these who are members of my family, you did it to me" (Matthew 25:40). "I was a stranger and you welcomed me" (25:35).

The presence of God that we meet in the stranger transforms people and communities into persons and groups of people who accept and affirm others of different religious and nonreligious traditions, conflicting cultures, alien psychological profiles, and socially confronting classes.

The research of Samuel P. Oliner and Pearl M. Oliner demonstrates the character of such people.[3] During World War II, when the Nazis were systematically torturing and killing Jews in Eastern Europe, ordinary citizens risked their lives to hide and to help these Jewish people. They had nothing to gain and everything to lose by helping anyone Jewish. If caught, they and their children would have been killed.

The Oliners searched for and found the children of these helpers and interviewed them extensively. They recorded their findings in *The Altruistic Personality*. These people's family experiences were similar in many ways. Remember, they had nothing to gain by helping the Jews and everything to lose, except their integrity and character.

Those people have the following characteristics in common.

1. Close family relationships in which parents modeled caring behavior and communicated caring values.

2. Parents set high standards—caring for others for the other person's welfare and not for any personal reward. Parents modeled such behavior.

3. Dependability, responsibility, and self-reliance were valued because they facilitate taking care of oneself as well as others.

4. Failures were regarded as learning experiences, with the presumption of eventual mastery, rather than inherent deficiencies of character, intellect, or skill.

5. Children learned to trust people and thereby risk intimate relationships.

6. Persuaded that attachment rather than status is the source of basic life gratification, as they matured they chose friends on the basis of affection rather than social class, religion, or ethnicity.

7. Physical punishment was rare by the parents. Gratuitous punishment—punishment that serves as a cathartic release of aggression for the parent or is unrelated to the child's behavior—almost never occurred.

8. Because of their solid family relationships, those people who helped the Jews had internalized their parents' values.

The Oliners call these people altruistic—people who are unselfishly concerned for others for the others' welfare.

Those people welcomed the stranger; that is, they perceived the stranger, in this case the oppressed and persecuted Jews, as somehow a part of who they were. The persecution of the Jews was also an insult and deadly blow to the humanity of the privileged who were not targeted for persecution.

Welcoming the stranger, being open to and accepting of the humanity and worth of others who believe differently than we do, does not imply an acceptance of anything and everything. There are limits to the Christian's and church's acceptance of diversity.

In *Truth and Community* Michael Kinnamon emphasizes that the absence of love creates unacceptable actions and communities. "If such love is genuine," he writes, "it must abhor those things that thwart it. We are justified in being intolerant of all that destroys tolerance."[4] It is unacceptable to accept or ignore anything that denies love. Elie Wiesel said somewhere: "What hurts the victim most is not the cruelty of the oppressor but the silence of the bystander."

It is love's duty to embrace the stranger while fighting the enemies of human dignity, personal worth, and peace (shalom). "Tolerance does not require believing that all statements about something are of equal value and equally true. To have respect for another person is not the same as agreeing with the other's viewpoint no matter what it may be."[5]

Rosemary Radford Ruether captures the concept of the limits of tolerance and diversity with her "critical principle of feminist theology." Her definition applies to all people who are oppressed and marginalized because of their gender, ethnicity, political position, economic status, social class, or sexual orientation. The critical principle of feminist theology is:

> ...the affirmation of and promotion of the full humanity of women. Whatever denies, diminishes, or distorts the full humanity of women is, therefore, to be appraised as not redemptive. Theologically speaking, this means that whatever diminishes or denies the full humanity of women must be presumed not to reflect the divine or authentic relation to the divine, or to reflect the authentic nature of things, or to be the message or work of an authentic redeemer or a community of redemption.[6]

The presence of God creates within people a sensitivity to and concern for others, while at the same time holding to a basic ethic of attitude and action that refuses to compromise the value, dignity, and worth of persons. Christians believe that they have been reconciled to God through the Spirit of God revealed through Jesus the Christ. This reconciliation between God and humankind reflects the nature of the "world"—the ways of reality. "Strangers who are welcomed and affirmed in their differences are proof of that reconciliation. When we welcome strangers we welcome the messiah (Christ), the kingdom of God draws near and all things are possible—all things are made new."[7]

Even with this newness of life there are limits to our ability to be loving all the time. Reinhold Niebuhr writes of the "impossible possibility," which is Jesus' love ethic's potential for renewing life and the limits of thinking, feeling, and acting in love all the time with all people.[8]

However, the presence of God mediated through the community attempts to renew us intellectually, emotionally, spiritually, and morally. The community creates an atmosphere of empathy and compassion while defining the loving thing to do and challenging people to so live. Marjorie Suchocki expresses it this way:

> Each generation expresses anew the Christian conviction that God is for us. The immediate catalyst for these expressions may well be the preferred conviction that God is a force for love, trust, and hope in a communal world. The conviction carries with it a drive for expression, and the expression itself contributes to the creation of love, trust, and hope. God is for us: therefore we speak, create a tradition, and live as a community called the church.[9]

In *The Power of Myth* Bill Moyers describes the following incident.

> In Japan for an international conference in religion, [Joseph] Campbell overheard another American delegate, a social philosopher from New York, say to a Shiate priest, "We've been now to a good many ceremonies and have seen quite a few of your shrines, but I don't get your ideology. I don't get your theology." The priest paused as though in deep thought and then slowly shook his head. "I think we don't have ideology," he said. "We don't have theology. We dance."[10]

If it were only that simple; yet, there is some truth to the thought. As Birch and Rasmussen wrote:

> The meaning of the dance is in the dancing of it. The meaning of the Christian life is in the living of it. There is little reason to talk about dance or receive instructions in dance unless at some point we ourselves dance, or our understanding of dance lets us enjoy the dance of others. Like-

wise, there is little reason to discuss the Christian life unless that discussion enhances our living of it, or our understanding of those who do.[11]

This dancing-living of the Christian life in a postmodern era is our concern. The pluralism of the postmodern era is not new; our awareness of the many diverse cultures with many different rituals, customs, values, ethics, and mores is a gift from God. We belong to a global community, therefore our common humanity takes precedence over national, political, social, and religious identities.

We approach this exciting possibility for global identity "speaking the truth in love" (Ephesians 4:15), hoping to manifest the presence of God, not from the pulpit or podium, but from the confessional. This confession inspired by the presence of God is not a defense of an idea/ideal but the sharing of the affirmation of all that lives. So this process creates a quality of character that is motivated to try to do the loving thing—the altruistic act. Therefore, the stranger is welcomed by those aware that they too are strangers to others. In the encounter both strangers, ideally, are open to learn and grow from each other and usually choose:

- Relationships over rules
- Cooperation over competition
- Kindness over cruelty
- Compassion over "correctness"
- Community over both individualism and conglomerates
- Persons over property and profits

The above is sometimes made possible because the presence of God mediated through the community attempts to renew us intellectually, emotionally, spiritually, and morally. The community tries to empathize with people while confronting us with the idea/ideal of doing the loving thing.

Notes

[1]Milan Kundera, *Immortality* (New York: Harper Collins, 1990), p. 72.

[2]Darrell J. Fasching, *Narrative Theology After Auschwitz* (Minneapolis: Augsburg, 1992), p. 106.

[3]Samuel P. Oliner and Pearl M. Oliner, *The Altruistic Personality* (New York: The Free Press, 1988).

[4]Michael Kinnamon, *Truth and Community* (Grand Rapids: William B. Eerdmans, 1988), p. 112.

[5]William V. Pietsch, *The Serenity Prayer Book* (San Francisco: Harper, 1990), p. 13.

[6]Quoted by Donald K. McKin, *What Christians Believe About the Bible* (New York: Thomas Nelson, 1985), p. 148.

[7]Fasching, p. 125.

[8]Reinhold Niebuhr, *An Interpretation of Christian Ethics* (New York: Living Age Books, 1956), p. 109.

[9]Marjorie Hewitt Suchocki, *God, Christ, Church* (New York: Crossroads, 1984), p. 3.

[10] Joseph Campbell, *The Power of Myth* (New York: Doubleday, 1988), p. xix.

[11]Bruce C. Birch and Larry L. Rasmussen, *Bible and Ethics in the Christian Life* (Minneapolis: Augsburg, 1989), p. 9.

16

*Spouse Abuse: A Conspiracy of Silence**

It was eight-thirty in the morning. I was in my study at the church admiring my to-do list. A timid knock at the door interrupted my thoughts. When I opened the door Mrs. Sims was standing there. Her eyes were red and puffed, her shoulders slumped, and her hands were quivering.

After we greeted each other and were seated, Mrs. Sims began describing a relationship with her husband, who was a deacon in the church I served, that was difficult to believe. "He beats me," she whispered as if ashamed of something.

"What do you mean, he beats you?"

"He hits me with his fist, knocks me down, picks me up, throws me against the wall or a table and...and then he kicks me several times." She sobbed and sobbed and sobbed. She sobbed not so much as one who had been beaten physically, but as someone who had been abandoned or rejected or degraded. It was the cry of disappointment, much as one hears from a child who feels betrayed by a parent's love.

"He hits me mostly in the stomach, legs, chest; places that won't show the next day."

---

*This chapter appeared as an article in two journals simultaneously: *Lexington Theological Seminary Quarterly*, Volume 26, Number 1, January 1991; and *Mid-Stream*, Volume XXX, Number 1, January 1991. It is reprinted here by permission.

I listened to this sophisticated, professional person talk about a deacon, a respected citizen of the community.

"He's trying to kill me," she said.

"Do you mean that he is trying to beat you to death?"

"No! He wants to kill me, but make it look like an accident so he can have our five-year-old daughter."

"How do you know that?"

I listened while she described "accidents" that had almost killed her, the latest incident being a tire blow-out forty-five minutes earlier that occurred just before she was to enter an interstate highway. According to the service station attendant, the tire had been cut to cause a blowout at a high rate of speed. This was the final act that caused her to seek help. If she died her daughter would be raised by her brutal spouse.

"What should I do?" she asked.

"Do you have relatives or friends who live out of town where you can go?"

"Yes! In Louisville."

"Go home. Pack clothes for you and your daughter and leave town immediately, before Carl returns home."

She left the office. About thirty minutes later she phoned. "Brother Broadus, my pastor is here at the house. Carl called him. Brother Smith said I can't leave Carl, and that if I do leave him I will go to hell. He said I should stay home and try harder to make Carl happy. He said that's God's will."

"No!" I replied. "It is not God's will that you be beaten and for you and Jamie to live in constant fear. Tell your pastor I said that, and then you leave the house immediately before Carl arrives." She did. And I wondered why she lived with Carl and endured those beatings for *seven years*.

The most common response the church and community have made to battered women throughout history is reflected in the advice of Brother Smith. The church and societies have endorsed a "conspiracy of silence" about men's battering of women, which is a grossly unethical act of omission.

Throughout history there have been laws made by men about spouse abuse. Rosemary Radford Reuther uncovered the following information. "A decree of the Council of Toledo in A.D. 400 decrees that if a wife of the clergy transgresses his commands, the husband may beat his wife, keep her bound in their home, and force her to fast but 'not unto death.'"[1]

Later the "Rule of Thumb" principle appeared in British law which said that a man may not use a rod larger than his thumb to beat his wife. "Barbaric, archaic laws," one would say. On March 11, 1990, the Commonwealth of Kentucky legislature debated and *voted* to decide whether it is illegal for a man to rape his wife. Until that time, a man could rape his wife and she had no legal recourse.

In February 1990 a conference was held that addressed this issue of violence against women. It was a part of the World Council of Churches "Decade of Churches in Solidarity with Women," with the aim "to awaken the whole church to assure women the recognition that their struggle for full humanity is not only understood but also shared by men in the life of the Church."[2]

The following is a touch of what I learned at the conference and from more than twenty years of experience dealing with abuse in the family and church. Read a few more incidents of violence against women and relive your experiences with it.

When I was eight, nine, ten, eleven, twelve years of age my bedroom was about ten yards from Mr. and Mrs. Simson's bedroom. In the summer our windows were open in Jacksonville, Florida. Often late at night I would be awakened by loud cursing, crying, furniture being knocked about, and pleadings from Mrs. Simson. That would go on for what seemed an eternity. Sometimes the police would come to their house. Things would become quiet.

"Al, take it easy. Calm down. Now go to bed and sleep it off." Or, "Take a walk to cool off." The police would leave.

Often Mr. Simson would resume beating Mrs. Simson. I do not think Mr. Simson ever went to jail for beating Mrs. Simson.

As a child I wondered why Mrs. Simson put up with these beatings. Why didn't she do something? I asked myself. Nothing was done until one night when Mr. Simson hit Buddy, his son, who had become adult-size while no one really noticed. Buddy beat his father brutally. The violence escalated. I wondered, Why do Mrs. Simson and Mary Simson, her daughter, who was also beaten regularly, stay in that house of horror?

That was a long time ago. Update: Beacon Hill Road, Lexington, Kentucky, 2:00 a.m. The doorbell rang. It was the ten-year-old daughter of our neighbors and friends.

"Call the police," she said. "Daddy's killing mama."

While I put on my topcoat, dress hat, house shoes, and gloves, Catherine phoned the police. It was cold, so I drove the one block, parked in front of the house, and waited for the police. After four or five minutes it occurred to me that Carol could be killed before the police arrived. I dashed to the front door, opened the storm door, and rang the door bell. No answer. I rang the bell again. No answer. On the fourth ring, the door was yanked open. I stepped in the living room and quickly glanced at his hands to see if he had a weapon. No weapons other than his clinched fist. Our faces were about twelve inches apart.

"I've come to visit." Picture this: 2:00 a.m. A man dressed in pajamas, topcoat, dress hat, house shoes, and gloves saying to a neighbor, "I've come to visit!" (This procedure is *not* recommended.)

He stared at me for what seemed a long, long time. "I'll have nothing to do with this," he said as he retreated to the basement den.

I stood in the living room waiting for something to happen. Was he going after a weapon? Where was Carol? Suddenly I realized that I was interfering in a private, family matter, and trespassing on private property. I would probably be the only person to go to jail if more conflict occurred. Five minutes later, Carol appeared properly dressed, hair combed, with makeup neatly applied.

"Are you all right?" I asked.

"Yes" she replied. She was embarrassed. Carol was a professional person, a community leader in Lexington, an intelligent, assertive individual who caused things to happen. Yet she endured these beatings. I sat in a chair, and she sat on the couch. She talked about work, her daughters, Catherine, and our sons; she talked about everything but the subject—her letting Al beat her.

I wondered: why does an intelligent, confident, competitive, compassionate, strong woman stay in a marriage that abuses and humiliates her?

What do you think? Why do women stay in abusive relationships? Consider the following reasons:

1. They think they have nowhere to go. Moving back into their parents' house is often humiliating and not welcomed. A week in a friend's home with one's children can strain a friendship.

2. They do not have enough money to support themselves and their children. In addition to the estimated 30 percent cut in income (often more) after separation or divorce, the cost for lawyers is often high and the court proceedings slow.

3. They rationalize that the financial advantages of home, food, credit cards, and car are worth the beatings. Dr. Theodore Shapiro, editor of the *Journal of the American Psychoanalytic Association* and professor of psychiatry at Cornell University Medical College, points out that the period of rising tension and hostility between couples is frequently followed, after the abuse, by contrite reconciliation—which can have its rewards.[3]

4. Because they were raised in families where their fathers beat their mothers, these women assume that this is how people live; therefore it does not occur to them that they have

an option. In the *American Journal of Obstetrics and Gynecology*, Dr. Ronald Chez, M.D., writes:

> There are economic, emotional, and societal interdependencies and constraints for most women. There is also the relative predictability of the known versus the fear of the unknown, including fear of reprisal. There are also cultural and religious constraints, continued hope for change, and the fact that many women love the man who is the batterer.[4]

5. Abused women may stay in the relationship because they think they can change the man. Robin Norwood expressed the thought: "When we don't like many of his basic characteristics, values, and behaviors, but we put up with him thinking that if we are only more attractive and loving enough he'll want to change for us, we are loving too much."[5]

For additional details on why women stay in abusive relationships, see *Battered Wives* by Del Martin.[6]

One startling fact is that some women blame themselves for the battering. This self-blame is the result of the biggest con-game in the history of womankind, which is the societal and psychological condition that makes women responsible for men's moods, for men's emotional well-being. Wives are supposed to fix the world for their husbands. If something goes wrong at the office, or if a traffic jam throws a man off schedule, or if anything makes him unhappy, a woman is somehow to blame. The hostility evoked by failure, or disappointment, or guilt feelings gets displaced on the woman.

Can you believe that some women and some men believe that when a woman does not fix his broken world, it's her fault that he is unhappy?[7] So he beats her. Is this rare?

Marie Fortune, a United Church of Christ minister and director of the Center for the Prevention of Sexual and Domestic Violence, writes:

> Violence against women is a fact of life in the United States. It is the common thread of women's existence which binds us together across race, age, class, sexual orientation and

religious preference. This violence is not random; it is not accidental. It is directed at us by men, strangers or intimates, simply because we are women. Because of our gender, we are perceived to be available victims: powerless, vulnerable, deserving of abuse. Statistically, we are most likely to be assaulted by a family member or acquaintance: hence the most dangerous place for a woman to be is in a relationship.

Nearly one out of two women has suffered rape or attempted rape, one out of five wives has been a victim of physical abuse by a husband, 59 percent of battered women have been raped by the batterer, one out of three girl children is sexually abused before she is eighteen years old. Simply because of our gender, we are viewed as legitimate targets for male aggression and violence. Every woman carries either the fear of violence or the memory of violence in her life.[8]

Why do men abuse women? There are four general reasons, and many variations of the four.

The first reason men abuse women is that it works in many cases. It intimidates women. A beating is the punishment for not fixing a man's world. After the battering, the woman tries harder to please the man. She not only does not want to disappoint him, she is afraid to "make him angry" and she often believes it's her fault that he is angry. (Reader, I am not making this up!)

As absurd as it sounds, the second reason men abuse women is that beating a woman gives the batterer a sense of power. The rewards of "working off" feelings of anger, disappointment, or impotency give temporary relief from frustration and failure. Power, control, and self-esteem have been reported as rewards for beating up women.

The third reason men abuse women is that men can get away with it. In *Intimate Violence* Richard J. Gelles and Murray A. Straus contend that being arrested for family violence is relatively rare. In 1988 they wrote:

Our most recent national survey of family violence found that fewer than one in ten police interventions ended in the arrest of the offender. Thus, the cost of arrest, which is very real for public violence, is nearly nonexistent in cases of intimate violence and abuse.[9]

The fourth reason men abuse women is that much of society approves of the behavior. The battering of women by men has been called the "silent conspiracy." Marie Fortune points out that we detest the idea of battering women (and children) in the abstract but tolerate it in reality. The American idolization of individual freedom for Bubba contributes to the violence. The man proudly proclaims and believes that "It's my house and my spouse, my car and my kid, and what I do with them is my business and nobody else's." And the laws and actions of our good-ole-boy society say, "Nobody tells Bubba or George or James or Reginald what to do." It is still difficult for a woman to get justice in spouse-abuse cases. Can you imagine what would happen to a man who suddenly turned on his coworker and beat her in the office? He would get five to ten years in prison.

The fifth reason men abuse women is the social training that conditions us to believe that violence is a legitimate way to solve problems.

Violence is a part of our patriarchal system. We promote it, practice it, and praise it. We pay Mike Tyson ten million dollars to fight James "Buster" Douglas. We elected a president, at least partially, because he promised to be as violent as necessary to protect us from violent people. Incidentally, the most frequent violence against women by men occurs in the following vocations: most frequent, military personnel; next, police officers; followed by...clergy! Our patriarchal system discriminates against women, thereby endorsing violence against them physically, emotionally, financially, and sexually.[10]

What is the solution to men's abuse of women? We can start with men working with women to do justice to correct this gross injustice. Women working with men must address the systemic situations that perpetuate the problems. One consideration in this "attack" on systems is to realize that being "fair" in an unjust system perpetuates the system. That is the dilemma with which to wrestle when examining ways to change the rules of the establishment.

In the church to which I belong, one way we keep rebels (those who disagree with people in authority) in line is to say, "We must keep the covenant." Translated, that means "We must work together for the good of the whole"; the issue becomes who defines what is best for the "whole people"—the church. The answer is usually those in power.

Sometimes those in power perpetuate unjust laws and actions such as violence against women. It is reported that 3 percent of spouse-abuse cases involve women battering men; this too is unacceptable. "Boys don't hit girls," my father taught me, and "Girls shouldn't hit boys" and "People shouldn't hit people."

Of the people answering the ethics questionnaire, 25 percent claimed to try to live by the Golden Rule and use it to make ethical decisions. "Do unto others as you would have them do unto you." The Golden Rule is a difficult idea/ideal for most abusers to understand, because of their experiences as victims of abuse. Abusers do unto others as they were done unto. Most, but not all, abusers were abused by their parents. Parents pass to their children by word and *action* the ways to treat people.

What would we do if we applied the Golden Rule to this abuse problem? Following are some suggestions.

1. Locate, support, and use spouse-abuse centers. Help abused people escape from their terror and torture. Help them find some hope for a better life.

2. Help abusers get counseling when they decide to deal with their abusiveness. Some abusers can be helped by group therapy designed specifically for them.

3. Challenge and try to change our small and large sys-

tems, congregations, church judicatories, places of employment, and families. Wherever we have an ounce of influence we are called to use it for justice.

4. In your church or organization, organize workshops on family abuse.

For additional information and assistance, write to: Center for the Prevention of Sexual and Domestic Violence, 1914 34th Street, Suite 105, Seattle, Washington, 98103, and to your church judicatory.

Diane Eisler, in *The Chalice and the Blade,* describes two basic models for society. The first one is the dominator model, popularly termed patriarchy or matriarchy—the ranking of one half of humankind over the other. The second model is based on the principle of linking rather than ranking. It is a partnership model in which diversity is not equated with either inferiority or superiority.

It is possible to develop that partnership approach to living and working together, men working with women "to awaken the whole church (and society) to assure women the recognition that their struggle for full humanity is not only understood but also shared by men in the life of the church."[11]

We will never get it perfect, but we can make it better.

There are few happy endings to violence-against-women stories. Here is one.

Several years ago I was sitting in a restaurant having lunch. A woman approached the table and addressed me as Brother Broadus. She was from a special place in my life—a former pastorate.

"I just want to tell you that I am doing great," she said while smiling almost slyly. She described the job she enjoys greatly. She is a top executive managing several hundred people who conduct social programs to help people. Her daughter graduated from college and is a professional person.

"I have had a great, free, joyous life since we last talked twenty-four years ago."

She was the former spouse of a deacon in a church I served—Ms. Sims.

Questions for Reflection and Discussion

1. Untangle the overlapping of mores and morals by identifying which actions and thoughts are mores and which are morals in this case study.

2. Apply the four dimensions of ethics—ideas/ideals, emotions, actions, and motivation—to this case.

3. To this case study, apply your method for making ethical decisions.

4. What is your church or organization doing about this conspiracy of silence?

Notes

[1]Rosemary Radford Ruether, "The Western Religious Tradition and Violence Against Women in the Home," in *Christianity, Patriarchy, and Abuse*, edited by Joanne Carlson Brown and Carole R. Bohn (New York: The Pilgrim Press, 1989).

[2]This conference was co-sponsored by the National Council of Churches of Christ Commission on Family Life and Human Sexuality and the Center for the Prevention of Sexual and Domestic Abuse. The theme of the conference focused on Violence Against Women. While recognizing that men are sometimes victims of domestic violence, this chapter focuses specifically on the widespread problem of violence against women.

[3]Quoted in "Battered Wives" by Stephanie Harrington, *Cosmopolitan*, April, 1990.

[4]*Ibid.*

[5]Robin Norwood, *Women Who Love Too Much* (New York: Pocket Books, 1985), p. 1.

[6]Del Martin, *Battered Wives* (San Francisco: Glide Publications, 1976).

[7]For an interesting interpretation of this interpersonal dynamic see *Intimate Strangers* by Lillian B. Rubin (New York: Harper and Row, 1983).

[8]Marie M. Fortune, "Violence Against Women: The Way Things Are Is Not the Way They Have to Be," unpublished article. Also see her *Sexual Violence: the Unmentionable Sin* (New York: Pilgrim Press, 1983).

[9]Richard J. Gelles and Murray A. Straus, *Intimate Violence* (New York: Simon and Schuster Inc., 1988), pp. 24–25.

[10]For a passionate description of the patriarchal system and an emerging female system see *Women's Reality* by Anne Wilson Schaff (Minneapolis: Oak Grove, 1981).

[11]Diane Eisler, *The Chalice and the Blade* (New York: Harper and Row, 1988), p. xvii.

17

Making Ethical Decisions

As we get older, it seems harder to discard tired obsolete ethics. We, therefore, should love 'em for who they are and be glad we know them. We don't need to attack everyone, especially elderly parents, because they're wrong and we know better. We wouldn't have known better if they hadn't given us some tools with which to learn better ways.

Walter Johnson[1]

My response to my neighbor's battering his spouse and terrorizing his children was initially emotional. "Boys don't hit girls" is from my father's voice. Without thinking of my beliefs about violence, or the source of the original belief, or what the Bible or church said about such matters, I confronted my neighbor, hoping that would stop the violence.

My ethics research reveals that most people's response to situations demanding a quick decision reverted to what their parents taught them, instead of some calculated Christian response. After time to reflect, I know that my actions are supported by what I believe the Bible teaches about abusing people, and about the worth of each individual. Although it does not always live up to the ethical standard, my church (tradition) believes the same. By reading the Bible and other books, attending seminars, and conducting seminars, I have learned more about the subject and affirm my belief that ideally, "Boys don't hit girls," and have added that "Girls should not hit boys" and that "Big people should not hit little people," and "People should not hit people."

There is more to that ethical process than what appears on the surface. My experience preceded my belief in a God of love. The Bible was an Aha! experience for me. My parents loved me and I never doubted that, even when they punished me. From this early affirming environment, I felt and believed that the Creator was friendly, concerned about me, and wanted what was best for me.

Until we identify and accept the early influences in our lives we are a conditioned reflex to the ethical challenges we face. So after using all my authorities and evaluating early influences, I know why I stand where I stand on the ethical issues involving violence in the family, and will not be as shocked *if* I find myself again standing in a neighbor's house dressed in my pajamas at 2:00 a.m. and incongruously saying, "I've come to visit."

My ethical decisions are in the context of grace as the idea/ideal, and my emphasis on making ethical decisions involves people identifying and dealing with their early environment as well as their present idea/ideals, emotions, and authorities.

"I angrily exploded at my daughter when she was rude to her mother," explained Ralph. "My reaction was worse than her action, yet I believe children ought to be polite to parents and parents to children. The next morning I described to a friend what I had done and how guilty I had felt. The friend described the likely reason for my anger, then explained how we collect cannonballs of guilt feelings and resentment until one day the suppression value pops off and we blast the nearest person for not living like we were taught to live.

"I have been examining the roots of my ethical standards ever since. Some I have discarded and no longer feel guilty about when I violate the standard, while others I cherish as being a superior standard of living that I want to pass on to my children."

Having read this far, you have probably been examining your ethical standards, maybe exorcising some and celebrating others. People who are not open to growing spiritually and morally probably tossed this book into a trash bag several chapters ago.

Let us review and examine methods some people use in making ethical decisions. It is assumed that when we have time, we will ask and answer some basic questions:

1. What does the Bible say about this?
2. What does my church believe about this?
3. What has my experience been with this?
4. Considering all the above, what do I think is the Christian thing to do?
5. Most people seek the counsel of a friend or confidant.

Again, one person condensed the above:

- Is it Christian?
- Is it credible?

Other questions to ask and answer will appear later.

We need a foundation out of which we live and make ethical decisions. Some people find the following helpful.

1. List the ten most important things in your life. Earlier, you listed what you considered virtues. This is a continuation of the process of affirming our values. This tells us who we want to be and gives us clues to who we want to become. We may or may not be proud of our values. Compare these with your early do's and don'ts.

2. While identifying the ethical edicts from parents and other authorities, ask: is this an ethical issue or a more in my community that does not have moral implications?

3. Identify how you *feel* about the ethical edicts. The stronger we feel about an issue the more likely we are to seek authorities to agree with what we already believe. Following are feelings that affect how we make ethical decisions and tell us who we are and give us clues to who we would like to become.

Emotions—Feelings

Angry	Loving	Lonely
Hostile	Affirmed	Passionate
Guilty	Relieved	Comfortable
Fearful	Resentful	Sentimental
Compassionate	Insulted	Joyous
Sympathetic	Hurt	Victorious
Empathic	Used	Neglected
Sad	Nervous	Pitied
Foolish	Rejected	Other:

At times, we do not live up to our ethical standards and fall short of our ethical ideal. Following are some traps that trip us in the ethical search for a "better life."

1. The need for approval. Our need to be liked may be so great that we compromise our values to be liked by others. This is far more prevalent than I originally thought.

2. Fear of failure, which can cause us to cut ethical corners.

3. The drive to succeed, which causes some to ignore people and shatter relationships.

4. Compulsive competitiveness, which may blind us to other needs and hurts.

5. Fear of impotency, which may drive one to exploit others sexually.

6. The desire to be wealthy and powerful, which may cause us to toss our ethical standards out the window of our soul.

Following are additional questions and answers people use in making ethical decisions.

Mary asks:

1. Does my decision value the people involved?
2. What best serves the community?
3. What maintains my personal integrity?
4. What is the loving thing to do?

5. Have I weighed the options and outcomes?

6. What would Jesus do?

Phillip asks:

1. What serves the sanctity of life best?

2. What serves the community best?

3. What serves the interest of love best?

4. What maintains my integrity?

5. What actions will treat others as a child of God?

Sarah asks:

1. What am I thinking?

2. Whom am I thinking about?

3. What am I feeling?

4. How will the decision affect my family (or significant others)?

5. How will this affect others involved (coworkers, clients, etc.)?

6. How will this decision affect me (loss of income, guilt feelings, etc.)?

7. What do I *want* to do?

8. What *should* I do?

9. Which decision will cause me to *feel* good about me?

10. With which decisions will I live what I believe?

Samuel uses the following procedure:

1. Gather as much data as possible.

2. Find out what the Bible says about the situation.

3. Ask myself, What is the Christian thing to do? or What is the most loving thing to do for all interested parties: for self, the other person, or persons; and How will the outcome affect all interested persons? When the loving thing is done, it must be done unconditionally, if it is love.

4. I pray and meditate. I pray that God will lead me in the right direction and give me the strength to do what is right. I

do this because I realize that although the ethical decision may be the best decision, it is not always what I want to do. Rather, it is what I must do.

5. In making ethical decisions, I also try to look at the situation in light of the history, the social psychology, and the sociology of all persons involved to come to a better understanding.

Regardless of the methods we use or the questions we ask, the most important issue is the quality of our character. That character makes a difference in us and between us and others. For the Christian, life is in the dancing of it, which at its best reveals a Presence that affirms our worth and shares our soul. The great moments of life have been empowered by the Presence felt through Mr. Halneck, Betty, Catherine, Jesus, Martin Luther King, Jr., and others who would be embarrassed if I mentioned them.

"God is love, and those who abide in love abide in God, and God abides in them" (1 John 4:16).

Note
[1]From personal correspondence.

18

An Ethics Group: Guidelines

> You shall know the truth and it will make you flinch;
> then it will set you free.
>
> *(Author unknown)*

The Need to Discuss Ethics with Others in Groups

One of the problems in the church has been a tendency to pretend to be what we are not with the intent to deceive others. That kind of pretending hurts us time and time again. To hide that which makes us feel evil, guilty, sinful, and worthless will continue to cause us to feel evil, guilty, sinful, and worthless as long as we hide that which causes us to feel that way, because it reflects the fact that we have violated our ethical ideals. As long as we pretend to be perfect or more moral than we are, we will feel fraudulent and will fail in our search for a sense of salvation, *today*. (See chapter 13.)

So that act of omission of goodwill that caused our sin (separation from God) continues to contaminate our "grasp" for grace. Until we confess to someone—tell our story—and feel accepted as we are and not as we pretend to be, we are imprisoned to the past. An ethics group may offer such an opportunity to tell our stories.

The Purpose of an Ethics Group

The purpose of an ethics group is to create an atmosphere of openness, honesty, acceptance, trust, forgiveness, and compassion so that the presence of God may be experienced by people who are interested in "letting love be genuine."

Because ethics is a personal, interpersonal, and community concern, it is important to discuss, debate, and deal with ethical issues in a community of people—church class, group, or seminar.

As people in your group share their dos an don'ts from the past and present, tell their stories, and sometimes confess their moral dilemmas, they may experience the presence of God in them and between them and others. This is the ideal. We deal with the real as we strive for the ideal in our groups by telling the "truth in love."

Principles for an Ethics Group

1. Leaders must share their experiences of life at a level that will invite and encourage others to do the same. Leaders often begin by sharing a few of their do's and don'ts from the past and then describing how these admonitions still affect them. (Remember: "Boys don't hit girls"?) Leaders share their ideas/ideals, behavior, feelings, and agreements and disagreements with ideas expressed in this book in each group session.

2. Design the group sessions so that participants will feel free to share at a level comfortable for them. Do not coerce confessions. As people listen to each other over a period of time (weeks, months, years) some of them probably will tell more and more of their story. An outline of a sample seminar session follows.

3. Demonstrate a pastoral concern and personal interest in people's stories. People are interesting—much more interesting than most television programs.

4. In a religious setting it is helpful to open and close each session with a prayer. Some other settings may prevent this due to organizational policy.

Remember: We are trying to create an environment in which deep friendships can develop so that people will share their censored stories, thoughts, and feelings and feel accepted and affirmed as they are by God and people.

An Ethics Group Meeting

1. After explaining the nature and details of the group process, ask the people to share one or two do's and don'ts their parents and other adults taught. You, the leader, begin by giving a few of your do's and don'ts. If the people do not know each other, ask them to give their name.

Next, add your experience and questions pertaining to making ethical decisions to the "Introduction to an Ethic of Presence." Data from chapters 1 and 2 may be helpful with the introduction.

2. Distribute copies of the ethics questionnaire. Ask participants to write their responses to the first three questions. Have additional paper available. Give sufficient time for group members to write their responses.

3. Suggest that participants get into groups of three to five people to "select" (draft) someone to record comments and questions. Most people are more likely to talk about themselves to a few people than to many people. A smaller group gives everyone an opportunity to tell his or her story and raise questions. Questions and comments after each chapter have been used in group settings with much success. Try it; it works.

4. Reassemble the participants into one group. Ask the recorders from each subgroup to share their group's comments and questions.

Remember: All ideas, questions, and comments are valid, so listen with pastoral concern and interest.

5. The closing of a session may be a summary by the leader or an explanation of future sessions. For instance: "Next week we will discuss the last three questions on the ethics questionnaire. After answering the questions you may want to read chapter 17, 'Making Ethical Decisions.' Thereafter we will follow the chapters in order."

Since the questionnaire calls for each person to identify ethical issues and explore his or her way of making ethical decisions, responses to the questionnaire can serve as a basis for all future sessions.

Appendix

The 1995 January Interterm Class

Clyde B. Akins, Sr.

David Leonard Carpenter

Roger Calvin Channell

Philip Grayson Cullum, Jr.

Douglas Dwight Gerdts

David William Gross

Robert Stephen Heath

Thomas Clayton Hughes

Craig L. Jones

Lorna Jean Loeffler

John Tekermu McCauley

Guy Everett McCombs

Muhit Chandra Muchahari

Demarcus Mulbah

Jennyfer April Phillips

Ted L. Satterfield

Steven Alan Smith

William Michael Stump

Zsolt Szabo

Earnest Charles Walls

Sheron Smith Ward

Paula Lynn Warren

David Michael Woods

Rebecca Claire Zelensky